Going Through . . .

HOW GOD TURNS TRAGEDY INTO TRIUMPH

By Jodi Peppard-Latocki

This book is dedicated to those who supported, loved, encouraged, and assisted

me through a dark, difficult, and traumatizing season of my life.

Thank you for pointing me to Jesus in my *going through.*

CONTENTS

Introduction   5

1. Fight or Flight   12

2. *My* Golf Club   29

3. The Waiting   46

4. Broken   70

5. Control   92

6. Fill the Void   120

7. Prison   147

8. Eyes Wide Open   174

Conclusion   208

Acknowledgments   219

INTRODUCTION

Going through . . . We've all been *there*, right?! Or maybe you're *going through* right now, in this very moment. Well, before we get started, I want to thank you for hanging out with me, *right here*, in this book, *right now*, while you're *going through* what you're *going through*.

This book is a devotional, meant to draw your devotion to the One who knows you inside and out. It's also a journal, where I hope you feel safe, comfortable, and unrestricted laying it all out, in a sense, at His feet. It's something you can walk through privately, do intimately with a close confidant, or *go through* with a group of brave souls who are also *going through*, just like you. However you choose to proceed, I'm going too. I'm here for the entire ride, encouraging you along the way.

Please feel free to underline phrases, scribble in the blank spaces, write out your thoughts, pour out your emotions, and inscribe the questions you have lingering deep inside you. It's completely okay to leave your teardrops, coffee stains, and ink smudges on the pages of this book too! I understand: the *going through* is not easy to talk about. In fact, you may not want to talk about it at all. It hurts to *go through*. It's frustrating to *go through*. It inflicts all sorts of discomfort to *go through*. It's not something we look forward to or prepare

ourselves for. It's not fun or comfortable or easy to *go through*. However, it is a

part of life, so why not process our *going through* with honesty and conviction

and a *willingness* to discover God's perspective in our difficulties and challenges.

Going *through* might look like a divorce you're facing, a job loss, a dream

crushed, a broken relationship that's left you with a broken heart. It may be an

injustice you've encountered, an addiction you struggle with, a trial that's testing

your will, confronting your fight, and trying your faith. It could be a letdown, a

disappointment, or a failure you're facing. It may be a health concern or a disease,

a financial loss, the death of someone you deeply loved, or a situation that rocked

your world and shattered it to the ground.

It's that uncertain, uncomfortable, and painful season of *going through,*

where our emotions run high without clarity, discouragement feels as thick as fog

with no hope or direction or light in sight. It's an inconvenience and a detour we

never planned to take or an event we never chose to participate in while the world

continues to move forward and time marches on, leaving us to feel left behind.

I know, I know, the Debbie-downer reality of *going through* might be as

frustrating to read about as much as it is to *go through* in itself, but please be

patient with me and don't close this book quite yet, because the *going through* is *not* the end of the story, even though it *feels* like it might be. In fact, *going through* is just the opposite. It's a season and a transition. It's temporary and ever-changing (Hallelujah!). *Going through* is just that—it's a period, an experience, an encounter defined by a moment in time. Therefore, it *won't* last forever (Thank God!), even when it may *feel* like it will.

Going *through* is a part of life, whether we like it or not. There is no volunteer waiver to sign up and accept. And although *going through* is defined as something not long-lived, it is also important to understand that it has the potential to leave a lasting consequence—a result and an imprint on who we are and who we will become. Our *going through* influences our destiny. It can shake us or shatter us, make us or break us, give us clarity and insight, or invite confusion and doubt. It may leave us high and dry or strong and fierce, paralyzed and unmotivated or empathetic and compassionate, causing us to become in bondage to our fears or stronger in our faith. It is a defining time for each one of us, and when the dust settles, what we allow our *going through* to do *in us* is completely *up to us*.

That's why I'm here, writing this devotional. I've experienced the pains of *going through* as well as the goodness of God *in* my *going through*. So, as we walk this out together, my prayer is for you to know this: there is hope to be discovered in your *going through.* There is triumph to be found in the tragedy. God's miracles are intertwined in *your* story. As you follow along in *my* journey, my heart is for *you* to understand God's truths and promises for you in this season, God's insight that will result in something more beautiful than you can possibly imagine, even in the midst of your difficulty.

It is vital, as we continue, to understand that we do not *go through* anything (and I mean *anything!*) alone. The Word of God is very clear about this. So dust off your Bible and check out these promises as we begin this journey together: Psalm 23, Joshua 1:9, Deuteronomy 31:6, and Hebrews 13:5. These are just a few profound reminders in the Word of God of the *One* who *goes through* with you and with me.

I am grateful to know there is One who goes through with us. One who has already gone before us, sacrificing His own life for ours (Matthew 27–28, Mark 14–16, Luke 22–24, and John 18–20). One who understands the *going through* better than we do (Isaiah 53). One who has seen the beginning and the end (and everything in between!) and One who holds the entire universe and the understanding of it all (Ecclesiastes 3:11 and Hebrews 1:3). One who sees our ugly mess and doesn't run for cover. One who stands strong regardless of *our* stance (Isaiah 43). One who never leaves, never abandons, and never gives up

(Deuteronomy 31:6). One who is there in the aftermath. This *One* is the One and only, *Jesus*.

Although I discovered His presence when I ran the fastest and the furthest away from Him, He seemed not to be run off by my rude rebukes or my lack of interest in His compassion toward me. *He never stopped pursuing me or loving me or offering to help me.* In fact, He met me *exactly* where I was—messy, lost, fragile, and ugly. And yet He walked *with* me—fully devoted, with a steadfast love, in faithfulness and gentleness, holding me together with His love, kindness compassion, and truth, in spite of my pushback.

My *going through* story began on Sunday, October 27, 1996, when my world was flipped upside down. It's a story that's been very difficult for me to describe in detail without strong emotions getting stirred up. It's an encounter that's been tasking for me to articulate fully, even as I write this devotional twenty-six years later. But I'm humbled to share my story with you that reveals my raw and real struggle. Thank you ahead of time for your kindness and patience with me as well as for accompanying me through the difficult details.

As we start this journey, I want to be honest in letting you know, I don't have all the answers or the "top ten ways of how to *go through* a difficult circumstance," especially the understanding as to the "why" behind it all, but I do know the One who does. My hope is that this devotional, filled with my flaws and frustrations, transparencies and ugly cries, my zany sense of humor, and my personal encounters where God has brought me understanding and insight—along with the accounts found in God's Word of countless others who also had seasons of *going through*—will point you to *the One* who will meet you exactly where you are and fill you with everything you need in your *going through*. This is my life story. It is my journey in finding Jesus, the One who turned my tragedy into triumph.

As we begin, take a moment to take some deep breaths. Allow the Lord to prepare your heart as you journey through these pages. I want to encourage you to listen to "Dancing on the Waves," a song by We the Kingdom, as we commence. Absorb every word as Jesus invites *you* to see *Him* in your *going through*. Just rest in His presence as He fills you up. Open your heart to receive all He has for you while you put aside all distraction.

God's miraculous story of hope and triumph can be found in the tragedy of your *going through*.

I pray that God, the source of hope, will fill you completely with

joy and peace because you trust in him. Then you will overflow

with confident hope through the power of the Holy Spirit.

(Romans 15:13 NLT)

CHAPTER 1

Fight or Flight

My eyes opened slowly to the irritating sound of someone running down our household stairs. I looked through the blinds of my bedroom: it was still dark outside; morning had not yet arrived. I remember thinking it sounded like a herd of elephants stampeding through the house. My room was pitch black as I tried to adjust my eyes to the wakeup call I never asked for. Seconds later, my mom's cry rang out like a siren outside my bedroom door. As I leaped out of bed, I recognized that something disturbing did in fact just happen.

I opened the door to find my mom repeating herself as she paced the hallway, back and forth. "Someone just shot your dad! Someone just shot your dad!" She repeated it over and over again as I stared at her in shock and disbelief. My irritation grew with my confusion, wondering what happened that had interrupted my sleep way too early and way too dreadfully.

My brain finally caught up to the scene I was standing in—without a caffeine fix—as if I were a character in a thriller movie. I became awake and alert to my strange surroundings. There was an eeriness and a violating sense about what I was seeing. I noticed immediately that every light in the house was turned on, like the brightness of an airport during the week of Christmas, as my mom rambled on, and my eyes slowly shifted to my parents' bedroom. Their door was open, and the light cast shadows into the hallway, but my ears still rang from the frightening sound of the trampling steps down the stairs and my mom's screaming. I was hoping in that split second, while I slowly moved toward my parent's bedroom, that my mom was actually sleep talking, rambling on and on about something that hadn't really happened. I took a deep breath in and sighed as I stepped closer to their bedroom door.

As I entered the room, the reality of this nightmare proved to be true. My dad was thrashing back and forth on my parents' queen-size bed, groaning and moaning in anguish and pain, while blood sprayed and spewed all over the bedsheets. I felt helpless, hopeless, and frozen, as if time had transitioned into a pause. My eyes tried to make sense of the sight, while my brain made the effort to adjust as well. I stared at him. I was speechless and paralyzed; tears filled my eyes, shock clutched my heart, and pain grieved my soul.

Memories seemed to flash quickly through my thoughts while I stood in shock. My *father*, our family's strength, provider, and protector, the one who raised us with love, character, and discipline. The man who reflected Jesus greater than anyone I had ever known. My *dad,* who fixed our hair with cockeyed ponytails and various-colored barrettes each morning before elementary school. The one who made our weird lunches: bologna sandwiches and pickles, with potato chips crushed between the bread. My *daddy*, who made the best spaghetti dinners, adding swirls of maple syrup to the sauce, before the movie *Elf* was ever made. The one who never missed a day without giving each of us a hug. The one who cried when we cried and the one who listened when we needed to be heard. I watched in desperation as He writhed uncontrollably before me. I felt helpless and powerless, but I knew I had to move. I knew I had to do *something*.

Fight or flight. I remember hearing this term in psychology class many times before. I'm sure you've heard it too. It's how we naturally respond, as humans, in stressful or difficult situations. It's not as if one response is worse than the other, but it does reveal and reflect something about us that we wouldn't have known otherwise. It is our natural reaction where our innermost being chooses *how* to respond to difficulty: to resist or to run away.

Life has a way of bringing about these opportunities to fight or take flight. And our *going through* is the perfect testing ground. Well, this seemed to be my moment. My fight-or-flight opportunity that I never got to rehearse or practice or even raise my hand to volunteer for. It was my moment of truth. A moment of decision. To fight or to take flight.

I quickly realized my response to this dreadful scene meant life or death for my dad, but it also meant something for me *personally*. I had always been a fearful person, running from tough stuff and avoiding challenges. However, in this moment, I knew I needed the One who could take me through, in spite of who I thought I was. I knew this moment confronted everything in me that I had buried: anxiety, insecurity, doubt, pain, and feelings of worthlessness. It was a defining moment that would reveal my weakness and thrust me into a moment of decision and an opportunity to surrender to God.

Jacob faced this too. Fight or flight. His story can be found in Genesis. It is one of my favorites, mostly because I can relate with his struggles, insecurities, and selfishness. (Anyone else with me?!) His story begins in Genesis 25:24 when he was born. I want to encourage you to check it out *right now*. As you begin to read in Genesis 25–31. Pay close attention to Jacob's decisions and actions, as they reflect his habits and lifestyle. What do you see?

____

____

____

What stands out to you about him? _____________________________

Is Jacob someone you'd want to call a close friend or a brother? ____________

I doubt it, but keep reading. It seems as though the apple didn't fall far from the tree as you read on, right?! His motivations reveal his personal self-interest. Lying, stealing, tricking, deceiving, and making self-absorbed choices would bring him what he wanted, for himself, when he wanted it. Can you relate? I know I can. We all have our own battles and challenges that we sometimes choose to face with our own self-interest in mind.

Jacob's *going through* season, as revealed in God's Word, seemed to be an *ongoing* battle through a few chapters in his life. Moments of stress and fear that challenged his innermost soul to decide to keep running or to fight for *something*. As we continue on, Jacob's trickery and scheming caught up with him as he faced the hatred and anger of those he'd deceived with his own personal gains and selfishness. Yet, according to Genesis 31, in the midst of Jacobs's conniving, calculating, selfishness, and constant running, the fact of the matter is, the Lord *remained* with him.

Jacob finally arrived at a moment of decision in Genesis 32:24. It appeared that God showed up to wrestle *with him*, not the other way around. His final fight-or-flight encounter was now upon him. Would he keep running from his issues? Would this, in fact, be his legacy? Or would he face the music and fess up and fight for something better? I encourage you to pause here and read it for yourself before we venture further through Jacob's story.

Jacob stood in a moment of truth. (I wish I could've heard his thoughts.) God before him, in the form of a man. I've pondered a few times, *I wonder how long they stood and stared at one another. Was this scene like an episode of* Gunsmoke, *where they wait for the draw?!* He now stood *face-to-face* with the One who could change it all, but it would require a match. A fight that would confront everything ugly within him: fear, insecurity, doubt, selfishness, and the reason behind the constant running.

This fight had nothing to do with who would win, mind you, because we all know who the winner really was. No, this fight had everything to do with God wanting something from Jacob. But what?! Jacob seemed to have nothing good to give (we may feel this way in our tough times too). But maybe that's the beauty of it. God wanted Jacob, *all* of him—his garbage lifestyle of selfishness, scheming, and conniving—and God was *willing* to show up, exactly where Jacob was (in his hot mess) and take it by force.

Jacob responded to God with a stance that said no more running, no more taking flight. His heart appeared to shift with his prayer of humility in Genesis 32:9–12. His fear led him to this prayer of remembering God's promises; it looked as though Jacob seemed to be done with his mess, while he recognized his need for a breakthrough, a change, a transformation. He was desperate. He knew it was now time to fight—to wrestle with God Almighty. This fight was *his* defining moment of decision: he could choose to let go of *all* control and get real with the One who *is* in control or continue with his self-seeking desires to have his own control.

The wrestling match with God went all night long. I would have loved to see it (popcorn in one hand and a Diet Sunkist Orange in the other) and listen to the comments exchanged between the two—if there were any comments at all! I imagine God asking Jacob with sincerity, while holding an anaconda squeeze around his neck, "Are you sure you're ready to be done with all of this?" God bringing a powerbomb next. "Do you really want everything I have for you?" Then God leading into a front headlock. "If you are, quit running from everything you fear and receive my grace for you!" Atomic leg drop with the atomic bomb-dropping questions while Jacob mustered up a powerslam to show he meant business.

The fight continued until morning. Facebusters, Boston crabs, piledrivers to the face until the sun came up. And then, all of a sudden, the fight ended. God touched Jacob's leg and put it out of joint (we'll call this move the God dejointer, just for the fun of it!). The touch brought the win of the match, and it went to God, of course (we knew that). Although Jacob's fight started off with his own self-reliance and personal strength, it ended with God conquering him completely. Jacob couldn't fight any longer, but God also recognized that Jacob would not let up as Jacob continued to cling to Him. In the past, Jacob had felt he was clever enough to get what he wanted; his self-reliance was now surrendered as he cried out to the Lord, "I will not let you go. You must bless me" (Genesis 32:26 ERV). Jacob's desperation and defeat brought him to a new understanding: he must cling to God because God was the One who was his hope in his *going through*.

This next moment is interesting, so pay close attention. God asked Jacob his name (Genesis 32:27), which I've always found funny, because we all know God already knew Jacob's name, especially after God was with him throughout his life (see Genesis 31). Chapter after chapter, and now after an all-night WWE battle where the headlines made it into the bestselling book of all time, it was obvious God *thoroughly* knew Jacob (his hot mess and all!). So why do you think God asked Jacob's name?

____

____

____

Genesis 32:28 (ERV) provides God's response: "Your name will not be Jacob. Your name will now be Israel. I give you this name because you have fought with God and with men, and you have won." I've come to believe God asked him his name *after* the match because it was necessary for Jacob to recognize who he used to be *before* this fight and to understand who he was *now*, after this incredible encounter with God Almighty—the One who gave him a new name and a new future. The One who essentially said, "Stop running. I'll meet you exactly where you are, in your darkest moment. I'll fight to have all of you, mess and all. I'll exchange all of me for all of you. I'll cling to you; will you cling to me?"

In that place, God *blessed* Jacob, because it was clear God's presence was *with* him. Jacob's true enemy—his prideful, selfish nature—had now been conquered by God Almighty. Jacob's new name, Israel, revealed a whole new meaning: God rules. In that moment of decision, Jacob's life was forever changed because of a fight: a match that caused him to see that God was all he needed to cling to in the *going through*.

What about you? Where do you find yourself in your *going through*?

What has been your *natural* response to the difficulty and stress you're facing right now, to fight or to run? ____

Have you been avoidant *or* are you willing to take a stance and confront your

need for His will in your *going through*? ________________________________

Esther had her moment (Esther 4:10–14), Joshua had his (Joshua 1:1–9),

and believe it or not, Jesus had His in Gethsemane (Matthew 26:36–39). If you

find yourself in a similar crisis, this is *your* moment. Your moment of decision.

Like Jacob, sometimes it's that fight in us that takes us directly to the feet of

Jesus. This is your fight-or-flight opportunity that will define your next steps in

your *going through*. Are you willing to allow God's will to take all of you by

force?

Reflection Questions:

Let's continue this devotional with the most important question, the reason you started this book in the first place: What are you *going through* right now? It may be multiple things you are facing or just one heavy-duty trial. Write it all down right here:

____

____

____

____

____

____

____

____

____

____

____

____

It's time to get real. Are you ready? _______________________________________

How have you been handling this *going through* season? Emotionally, mentally, physically, and spiritually? Be honest as you fill the lines with whatever words come out to describe what you are experiencing. Describe how you're responding and where you are in this journey.

____

____

____

____

____

____

____

____

____

____

Has this season sent you in flight, running from the pain and trying to avoid it?

Talk about it here.

____

____

____

____

____

____

____

____

____

____

____

____

Are you willing to take a stance today, to stand your ground in faith—willing to trust God to have His will be done in the midst of your *going through*? Share your thoughts.

____

____

____

____

____

____

____

____

____

____

____

____

Can I encourage you to do something before you move forward in this devotional? Take a few minutes to listen to "As You Find Me," a song by Hillsong UNITED. If need be, listen numerous times. What do the lyrics speak personally to you? What is the Lord revealing to you about who He is in your *going through*?

____

____

____

____

____

____

____

____

____

____

Going through difficult times will always reveal more about ourselves than we anticipate, *but* it will also reveal more about who God is and His willingness to meet us exactly where we are in our pain. In our fight-or-flight moment, as we repent and take hold of His promises, a great exchange takes place (Isaiah 61:3): our mess for His joy. Cling to Him, don't let go. Jesus is faithful to be your hope in this season.

Rather, cling tightly to the LORD your God . . .

(Joshua 23:8 NLT)

CHAPTER 2

My Golf Club

After the disbelief wore off from seeing my dad in such despair, I began to recognize the adrenaline coursing through my veins. I *immediately* shouted to my mom, "Call 9-1-1! Call 9-1-1!" I watched her pick up the house phone, her ear pressed hard against the plastic earpiece and her face as pale as printer paper. She hung it up quickly on the receiver with confusion in her eyes and began to pick it up again and again and again, searching for the dial tone. But there was no dial tone to be found. The phone line was cut, and there was no way to reach the outside world from the nightmare we were in. It was becoming more apparent with each second that passed, the violator who wanted my dad dead had gone to great lengths to make his plan succeed.

Cell phones were a new thing in the nineties, mostly owned by businessmen, so we relied fully on old-school phone lines connected to our homes. Without a phone, the only logical thing to do next was for one of us to go for help. My mom, being a nurse, needed to stay. She could assist my dad medically, whereas my little sister and I could not. My mom grabbed the overwhelmingly large metal ring of church keys and began probing for the exact key I needed to enter the church. My dad was the senior pastor of our small-town church, and it was literally just up our driveway, about a thousand feet from our home. Our home was nestled on three acres of land, with over eight acres of trees, fields, and wildlife surrounding us. I thought to myself, *If I can just get to my dad's office inside the church and use the phone to call for help, my dad can survive this.*

My mom continued to fumble through the ring of keys when I noticed my little sister, Leah, sitting on the stairs, frozen and paralyzed by the chaos around us. She had just woken up to this disaster, and I could see she was *going through* the same agonizing motions my mom and I had already *gone through.* She had turned seventeen days before this trial, and though my heart wanted to console her like a big sister should, I knew I had to stay focused on getting out and getting my dad help.

I grabbed the enormous ring of keys from my mom. I couldn't wait any longer. I began to feel the adrenaline pump harder and harder in my chest, and I felt a sense of anger toward whoever had done this to my father and my family; it began to frustrate me and boil my insides. My mom started to speak motherly advice with clarity and concern as I made my way to the garage door, slipping my feet into the first old pair of shoes that I could find. With keys in hand, I heard my mom call out, "Be careful, honey. I love you. Please be careful!" I yelled back, "I love you, too, Mom. I will!" Not sure if I would see my dad alive again or see anyone else again, for that matter.

My uncertainty while leaving caused me to feel the need to tell my dad exactly how I felt about him. I yelled with emotion and intent, hoping my words would echo to his upstairs bedroom and keep him hanging on for dear life while I was away: "I love you, Dad. Please don't die. Please don't die. I love you so much and I need you."

Tears welled up in my eyes. Righteous anger fueled my steps. I felt a sense of vigor and might fill me. I knew it was time to face the unknowns of the outside, and I knew someone greater was giving me the courage and strength to do so, because there was no way I could do this alone.

I opened the door that led into our garage. It was the entry I used to come in and out of the house every single day—through *that* garage. As I cautiously swung open the door, the light in our garage shined brightly, and I knew it was left on by the trespasser, just as *all* the house lights had been left on throughout our home. The first thing I saw as I entered the garage were my dad's golf clubs. They were stacked, standing straight up in my dad's golf bag.

To be honest, I know absolutely *nothing* about golf. In high school, I would play golf with my dad occasionally because I knew he enjoyed it and I enjoyed being with him. We would walk the course while others rode around on golf carts, and we would laugh at any chance we had to yell, "Fore!" I wasn't any good at the sport, but my dad didn't seem to mind. We just hit golf balls, talked about life, laughed over funny things, and grabbed lunch on our way home.

As golf memories ran through my mind, I grabbed the first golf club that I could reach for from my dad's bag. I'm not sure if it was a nine iron, a wedge, or a putter, but it really didn't matter to me. This wasn't golf. This was life or death for my dad. I knew his life was hanging in the balance, and this golf club suddenly became *my thing*, my weapon, my lifeline, my protection, and my *only* hope. I clung to it like my life depended on it, holding it like a bat, ready to defend myself and my family from whoever or whatever I was about to face.

I glanced around the room at all the elements inside the garage that early morning, not sure if the intruder was there awaiting my arrival. *Is he hiding behind a cabinet or maybe the tool chest?!* My eyes raced around the room with questions. Our garage was used for storage, so I prepared my mind for whatever could be camouflaged among the clutter. After I inventoried the space, it appeared to be safe, so I took the next steps that would lead me to the outside door, uncertain of what I might face out there.

It was roughly five a.m. I knew the sky would be pitch dark and the air crisp. It was late October in Michigan, so there was even a chance of a blanket of snow or a layer of fog. Uncertain yet persistent, I held my golf club as my security, safety, and protection, making it *my* source of strength for my next steps.

Have you seen *The Lord of the Rings*? I'm sure you have. The entire movie is centered around the gold ring, known by all to be a source of power. The ring is enticing but brings bondage to the individual who holds it, enslaving the owner who wears it. Its draw is manipulative and addictive, transforming pure and wholesome hearts into dark and greedy ones. However, the ring brings a sense of security and strength to the individual who clings to it. It is often called "my precious" by one character, Gollum, who finds it and hoards it, because without it he feels lost, unsure, and insecure. Well, that's what this golf club became for me. *My precious. My golf club.*

This golf club became *my* security, even in the aftermath of this event. I kept it close during many sleepless nights filled with fear, pain, and worry, believing this horrific event could reoccur; I held it like it was my *only* chance of survival. My security blanket. My golf club. My "one thing" that could get me through this terror and trauma.

My golf club became *my* crutch. The thing I thought I needed to protect myself and my family. The weapon I clung to "just in case." The item I needed to have around or my mind would panic and freak out. It became *my* dependency, *my* safety, and in my mind, it kept me safe and sound.

You may be reading this with a giggle in your gut, thinking, *How silly! A golf club?! Your protection and safety?!* But the downright truth is, when any of us are *going through* a difficulty, we all tend to look for that something or someone to be that "one thing" that brings us the security we need to get us through. It's a codependency on something or someone we rely on. We look for the safety we're craving and the comfort we're desiring, and we will look for anything within our grasp, out of desperation, even something as stupid and silly as a golf club.

Now your "thing" might not be a golf club; it may be a substance, an action, a secret activity; it might be someone or something you need to have close by so you can *feel* in control; it could be busyness or isolation or a dysfunctional attachment to a person, place, or thing. It may even be something that doesn't seem unhealthy at all. Well, whatever it is, and as silly or as serious as it may seem, that "thing" can become a shackle of bondage, a crippling dependency that you rely on to get you through your *going through* without you even realizing it.

As you continue to read my story, is the Lord bringing awareness to the "golf club" you are clinging to in *your* difficult season? If so, who or what has been your safety and security? There could be one, two, or a few; please feel free to be honest and sincere with yourself and God as you write them here:

____

____

____

____

____

____

____

____

____

I've learned that the Lord loves our willingness to be truthful with Him (1 John 1:9 GW). He already knows us inside and out, but when we take the next step to confess them with sincerity, repenting of our dysfunctional attachment, and a willingness to surrender them, He is faithful and reliable to become the One thing we really need.

Luke 10:38–42 has become a special story in my life, one that I read often. It grounds me and centers me, bringing me back to where I'm meant to be, especially when the winds of *going through* stir things up. Because we live in a fallen world full of quick fixes, we can easily grab hold of the easiest and most attainable "golf club" to get us through the challenges we face, when all along there is really just One who can do it all and wants to be our focus and our fix. The One who really satisfies.

This story reminds us of Him, the One who wants to walk us through the *going through*. Please join me in turning to this simple yet powerful account in Luke. As you read, you can see the story unfold. Join me as we join Martha who invited Jesus to be her guest at her home one afternoon.

I like Martha. I can tell she was a doer and a get-it-done kind of person. She's the kind of person I'd call if I were throwing my best friend a surprise party or putting together a special event. And for those of you who are amazing at hospitality, like Martha, I can only imagine your planning and preparations for those special events. The long hours, the yummy food prep, the cleaning, and the little details involved, but just imagine the thought of Jesus, the Son of God, the King of the world, coming over to *your house.* I have a feeling your hospitality game would be taken to a whole new level, and it's obvious Martha's did too.

While Martha polished and prepped, planned and prodded throughout the house, trying to get everything in perfect order, her sister Mary sat at Jesus's feet in adoration, listening intently to every word He spoke. She was enthralled by His words and His stories; she seemed to be laser fixed on Him, and nothing could distract her or pull her away, not even her agitated sister's footsteps running rampantly around the house.

As beautiful as Mary's actions were, our flesh can't help but shift to Martha's dilemma as we feel sympathy for her. She was just trying to get things done so she, too, could rest and listen, right?! I know what you're thinking, because I'm thinking it too. We all feel for Martha because we've all been in her shoes. Those situations where we are doing it all, running around frustrated, while that other someone just sits and does nothing and we're thinking in judgment, *If we don't get it done, who will?*

Martha became agitated (understandably) and most likely passive aggressive (like we all do at times). I imagine her slamming cupboard doors and sweeping the dust on the floor toward Mary, just to get her sister's attention and to show her annoyance (we all know how sisters can be). I can only envision Martha's self-pity and sense her victimized thoughts (because I've had them too): *I wish I could just sit at Jesus's feet, but I don't have time, because I have so much to do!* In fact, Martha's irritation even caused her to tell on her sister and blurt out to Jesus, "Tell her to help me" (Luke 10:40 GW).

Before you start cheering Martha on for taking a stand for herself, pause and think about this story with me. Picture yourself there. Hindsight is always twenty-twenty. Let's keep it simple and answer these few questions. Who was in their home? ________________ What was Martha focused on? ________________ What was Mary's attention on? ________________ Who seemed to be focused and fixated on what really mattered, especially in that moment? ________________ And why do you believe this?________________

____

____

____

____

It's amazing what happens when we simply pause and reflect: we can see the truth crystal clear. Martha's intentions and focus weren't a bad thing; in fact, she meant well, wanting to prepare and prep for Jesus's visit. But when we stop and contemplate this scene, removing the distractions, it's obvious that Martha was missing out on something (and *someone*) very special that was right in front of her. It was *who* and *what* she needed most.

Luke 10:41–42 (GW) says, "The Lord answered her, 'Martha, Martha! You worry and fuss about a lot of things. There's only one thing you need. Mary has made the right choice, and that one thing will not be taken away from her.'" Martha's issue wasn't with Mary or even trying to get Jesus to get her sister to help; her real issue was her own distractibility.

Martha was caught up with what she *thought* was important. The thing she *thought* would bring her peace, rest, and fulfillment. Her busyness and accomplishing was *her* "golf club." It became her disruption from the One thing that would provide exactly what she really needed, and she literally almost missed it. The One thing she wanted and needed most was sitting right there in her house, fully available, right in front of her, ready to be her everything.

Reflection Questions:

As you reflect on Martha and Mary's story, imagine yourself in their home.

Where do you see yourself in that story? Who are you most like and why?

____

____

____

____

____

____

____

____

____

____

____

Ponder for a moment Jesus's words about Mary in Luke 10:42 (GW), "There's only one thing you need. Mary has made the right choice, and that one thing will not be taken away from her." How does hearing Jesus talk about Him being the One thing we really need speak to you in your *going through* season?

____

____

____

____

____

____

____

____

____

____

There are various scriptures that speak of the "One thing" throughout the Bible. Take some time to study them; then write them down below, considering how you can apply them to your life: Psalm 27:4, Luke 18:22, and Philippians 3:13–14.

What "golf clubs" or other things are distracting you from the "One thing"? Are you willing to lay them down for who you really need in your *going through*?

As you spend time with Jesus, take a moment to listen to "Give Me Jesus (You Are My One Thing)" sung by UPPERROOM. As you listen and rest in His presence, I want to encourage you to open your heart to receive Him as your One thing. Write down what He is saying to you.

____

____

____

____

____

____

____

____

____

____

____

Going through will entice us to grasp at anything or anyone for security, safety, and comfort to get us through our *going through,* bringing distraction and disruption from time with the One we really need: our One thing. Our One thing is Jesus, and He will be your everything if you let Him.

Come close to God, and God will come close to you.

(James 4:8 NLT)

CHAPTER 3

The Waiting

I slowly opened the side door of the garage and glanced around. The outside world did not welcome me with sunshine or warmth. My house was surrounded by complete darkness and a blanket of fog that blinded me from seeing past a few steps. I wasn't sure what was ahead of me or beside me; I just began to take large steps toward my car and to shout without thinking. My words leaped out like weapons as I spewed insults at the intruder, as if he were standing right in front of me. For some strange reason, shouting at him in that moment made me feel strong, but the truth is I couldn't see a thing, and inside I was trembling like a leaf. My words released my rage like darts aiming for their target as the adrenaline coursed through my body.

I continued to grasp my golf club like a bat, ready to take on or take out anything that came near me. I felt feisty and ready to unleash my anguish. My eyes shifted, and my body turned in every direction, keeping watch all around me. I knew my car sat in the field ahead of me, at least twenty feet from the house. Everything around me felt eerie and uneasy, as the cold air and intense fog enclosed me. I felt like a character in a horror film, where the viewers painfully cover their eyes in embarrassment, watching the ridiculous dumb girl act tough while the viewer thinks she's an idiot for going outside. I knew *nothing* could have fully prepared me for this moment.

My hands shook as I reached my vehicle with my keys. Standing still next to my gray Topaz caused my body to feel more anxious than I felt while stampeding and yelling into the dark, hazy sky. Once I opened the door, I jumped in and looked around to be sure no one was hiding inside. I locked the doors quickly, started the engine, and turned on the lights. The mist brought a whole new level of strangeness to the scene as I peered through my windshield.

I put my car in drive, revved the engine, and accelerated down my winding, dim, and obscure driveway. I trembled at the thought of the intruder stepping in front of my vehicle with his loaded weapon to stop me. My mind had accepted that this person was so intent on killing my dad that morning, he went through the trouble of cutting the phone lines and shot my dad while we all slept. I didn't put anything past this impostor. I knew he was willing to do *anything* to stop me from getting the medical attention my dad needed.

Every branch from a tree that swayed in front of my car and every bush that rubbed against the doors startled me, yet I felt God's hand leading me through the unknowns of this haunted trail called my driveway. When I finally reached the church parking lot, I looked across the vastness before me. My intent to call 9-1-1 from the church was suddenly disrupted when I could see plainly that the lights were left on in the hallway of the church. *This prowler has a thing with turning on lights and leaving them on.* Immediately I felt a check in my gut not to go there. My dad was always a stickler about locking up the church and making sure the lights were turned off after everyone left, so this view caught me off guard and kept me pursuing a new route for help.

The night before this horrendous morning, my older sister, Jen, was married in our church. It was a beautiful occasion filled with celebration, laughter, delicious food, and a time of togetherness with family and friends. Jen gleamed with happiness while my little sister, Leah, and I stood proudly as her maids of honor. The fall colors of the Midwest and our burgundy bridesmaid dresses accented Jen's exquisiteness as a bride. I was so proud of my big sister and the joy she had found in marrying her best friend and college sweetheart, Joe. The two made the most beautiful bride and groom as they stood madly in love on the platform before God and all of us.

My dad and Joe's best friend, Rob, officiated the wedding, bringing humor, fun, and sweet sentiments to the service. I cried as I listened to their vows and the realization that my big sister was now stepping into the role she had always dreamed of becoming: a wife and one day, hopefully, a mother.

As I continued to roll past the church with the discernment of not stopping, my eyes watered and my stomach sank thinking about the shift from joy we felt the night before to the horror brought on by the morning. I slowly approached the main road to exit the church lot. I had two options, to turn right or turn left, either way with the determination to find help. I had no wisdom or understanding or any insight, for that matter; in fact, I was only taking each step with God's grace, and I was desperate for *His* direction. Immediately, I felt a tug in my gut to turn right and head to a person's home I had cleaned for who lived nearby.

Jen and I had started a cleaning business that fall, while she prepared for her wedding and I began my college career that same semester. It gave us a chance to be together and work, plus make some money for our life events taking place. One of the homes we cleaned for was approximately two miles away, and the family was one of the sweetest families we worked for. The wife was employed by our local police department as a dispatcher, and she was one of those lovely and kind people who left us sweet notes with candies and goodies each time we cleaned their home.

As I drove down the main road toward their house, the fog was just as thick as it was around my home. I knew the Holy Spirit was leading me, because my body was as frazzled as my thoughts and emotions were. However, I tried to keep watch for the intruder everywhere around me. I had no idea who he was, what he drove, or why he'd even done this. I just knew I had to be vigilant. My mind jumped to various scenarios, imagining his car pulling out behind me, chasing me down the unoccupied roads I traveled. I kept watch and stayed attentive. The only peculiarity I noticed that early morning was a white vehicle parked on the side of the road with clear access into the field where my house sat. I took a deep breath in, relieved and grateful I hadn't stopped at the church to call for help.

When I arrived at the family's home, I leaped out of my car and ran to their side door, the same door I'd entered each time I cleaned. I knocked and I shouted since my dad's life depended on it, hoping someone would wake up so I could call 9-1-1. It felt as though hours and hours had passed by since I was awakened by the stampeding down the stairs. I'm assuming trauma does this, making time feel like it has stopped or is going in slow motion. I continued to feel that *every* second that went by was a second closer to losing my dad, so I banged louder on the door and shouted in desperation.

My obnoxious knocking and yelling worked. The door sluggishly swung open as the husband and wife stared at me in confusion and hesitantly let me into their kitchen. I walked in like I owned the place, speaking sternly and loudly, "Someone shot my dad! I need to call 9-1-1!" I paced the floor swiftly. My mouth was dry, and my words were slurred as they encouraged me to sit down at their kitchen table; they handed me a glass of water.

In disbelief, they stared at me and pulled up a chair too. I could see they wanted to console me but questioned my sanity and my crazy-sounding statements. Their puzzled looks spoke louder than words. "What happened, Jodi?" the husband asked, but I didn't have time to answer and give details. I had no time to chat about what took place or how I was feeling about it or why I was even at their home at this early morning hour. I was only here on assignment: I needed their phone, and I needed to call for help.

They began to see and hear my urgency, so they dialed 9-1-1. They handed me the phone, and I found myself pacing again as I told the dispatcher the same alarming announcement. The dispatcher began to ask me all sorts of questions about what happened. I tried to explain the dreadful situation verbally for the first time, but I soon became out of breath and started spiraling into a full-blown anxiety attack.

Expressing the details of what I'd encountered that morning caused my brain to completely disconnect from my mouth. Everything I wanted to say spewed out differently. It was as if I was having a stroke and aphasia had taken over. The family sat me down once again and encouraged me to breathe slowly and drink water. The wife kindly took hold of the phone and began speaking with the dispatcher on my behalf.

This moment of the morning always gets a little challenging for me to share, because the anxiety I was experiencing literally paralyzed my words and immobilized me from the inside out. It was exasperating. I just remember, I wanted to communicate three things: someone shot my dad, he needs medical attention, and here's my address. Eventually, as I caught my breath and began to relax from the trauma, I was able to communicate more rationally.

The dispatcher stayed on the phone with the wife as I calmed down from the anxiety attack. But as soon as my mind relaxed, reality hit me like a slap in the face: I had no time to rest and self-soothe. I had to get back *immediately*. I blurted out, "I have to get home!" My senses instantly alerted me, and I jumped up from the kitchen table. I knew I had to see my dad *alive* and get back to help my mom and little sister.

The police dispatcher instructed the family to have me stay at their home. The police were on their way, but they felt concerned that the trespasser might still be in the area, armed and dangerous. My frustrations grew as I began to sob with sadness. I pleaded to go, stomping around the kitchen in desperation. It was maddening. I couldn't just sit there knowing the possibility: my dad could die while I was gone.

"Please, please, please!!" I begged. I cried like a two-year-old with separation-anxiety, in desperate need of her parents, pacing the floor back and forth, with all the reasons why I must get back. My heart sank to the ground as they refused to let me go. They tried to explain to me, logically, kindly, and calmly, why I had to wait.

The waiting became a large part of my *going through.* It is vital that you pause and address it in your season as well. And this seems to be the pivotal and vital moment to do just that.

That morning ushered me into a whole new level of the waiting game, and it seemed to last much longer than I would have ever desired. The waiting to go home that morning along with the season of waiting for answers to this traumatizing event caused much turmoil to my soul. It actually lasted years. It was torturous because I had not yet learned the beauty and truth of Isaiah 40:31 (GW):

"Yet, the strength of those who wait with hope in the LORD will be renewed. They will soar on wings like eagles. They will run and won't become weary. They will walk and won't grow tired."

I don't know about you, but *my* waiting did not feel like soaring; the running left me weary, and the walking was tiring. And during my *going through*, my entire world revolved around *waiting* for something. Something that I thought I needed to have immediately in order for me to start living again. Are you feeling that way too?!

I was completely missing God's intended view of this waiting season that revolved around this criminal act. I wanted answers and I wanted them now. Instead of discovering God's divine insight, perspective, and understanding, I was omitting His rest, strength, and vigor, and neglecting to wait with hope in Him. My world was wrapped around my need to find *my* understanding, not God's; I required a concrete answer of who did this and why it happened in order for me to accept what happened and move forward. And this seemed to be unattainable.

I felt as though I was in limbo. A constant state of uncertainty. The in-between left me feeling uneasy, unsatisfied, and just wanting to know the final outcome. *Waiting* to see if my dad would survive. *Waiting* to find out if the police would capture the intruder. *Waiting* to feel safe again. *Waiting* to heal from the pain and trauma. *Waiting* to move on. *Waiting* for life to just be normal again. And the truth is, this kind of waiting wore me out.

Waiting is never easy. As humans, we want, we need, we must have, and we must have it *now*. We don't like to wait. In fact, we're not very good at waiting even when life brings us butterflies and rainbows. The cold hard truth is, life requires us to wait; in fact, much of life is a waiting game. I don't know about you, but I've concluded that I want to follow God's way of waiting in the *going through* so I can accept His edification and identify the mystery that says there is something good to be found in such a time as this.

I knew there must be a way to wait that allows the Lord's peace and presence to lead and guide me while *going through*, and I was determined to find it. I eventually did in the life of a young lady in God's Word. She is one of my favorite women in the Bible, someone who possessed a quiet strength, like the strength described in Isaiah 40:31. She seemed to understand the waiting better than most, capturing the intriguing mystery of the *why* even when it didn't make sense. She seemed to capture the powerful truth that waiting on God silences self, allowing His voice to be heard and His hope to be seen as Psalm 62 speaks of.

If you want to join me in the book of Esther, we'll take a walk through her life. Please feel free to start in chapter 1 so you can better understand the entire context of this book. Esther, whose real name was Hadassah (Esther 2:7), was raised by her cousin Mordecai after her mother and father died. The start of her life began with her *going through* season, and I cannot imagine the pain of her waiting season during this difficult time. You may already be familiar with her life, but if not, her story unfolds in chapter 2 as she was one of many girls in the province of Susa who were chosen to go before the king so he could choose his next queen.

Esther, along with hundreds of other young women, would interview to fill the position of the last queen, Vashti. As you walk through chapter 1, you can see firsthand what kind of king it was who was looking at these young ladies' résumés. The queen's role seemed to be expendable—out with the old and in with the new.

It was a kingdom beauty pageant that would leave most of us ladies in a state of vain comparison, cut-throat competition, and strict self-criticism. Esther went through twelve months of beauty treatments in preparation to meet with this king (Esther 2:12). Can you imagine the uncertainty she faced during this waiting?! The thoughts that plagued her mind?! What if he did not choose her? What if she wasn't pretty enough? What if she didn't measure up? What if she failed? All the what-ifs can cause a young lady to feel insecure, worthless, and doubtful of who she is and her *true* purpose.

Well, a year of waiting went by, and it was now Esther's turn to meet with the king (are you feeling her butterflies?!). Esther 2:15–18 describes the details. She immediately found favor with all who met her, including King Xerxes who chose Esther to be his new queen. *Let's go, Esther!* It sounds like the perfect Disney movie, right?! However, Esther's story was not quite over, because being queen meant much more than just beauty pageants, following the king's orders, dressing up, and having a pretty face; it was also an opportunity to recognize and embrace God's timing and God's waiting.

Behind the scenes of this story was a corrupt man named Haman. Haman hated the Jewish people, especially Esther's cousin Mordecai. However, Haman had no idea that the new queen was related to Mordecai and that she was also Jewish (dun, dun, dun). As we continue reading, we see that Esther kept her nationality and family background hidden because Mordecai advised her to do so (Esther 2:10).

Chapter 3 brings the suspense and anticipation when Haman devised an evil plot to destroy the Jewish people. He manipulated the king's judgment and played off his pride, talking him into signing an executive order to destroy, kill, and annihilate all the Jews, including women and children, young and old, *in one single day.* When Mordecai learned of this edict, he grieved and lamented over it, along with all the Jews in the region.

It seems Esther was protected from the bad news and the broadcast alerts coming from inside the palace walls, but one thing she knew for sure was that her cousin Mordecai was grieving, and she wanted to understand why. She summoned him to tell her what was happening (Esther 4). Once word traveled to Esther, Mordecai urged her to go before the king and plead for their people's lives. In response, Esther sent a message back to Mordecai reminding him of King Xerxes's law stating that she could be put to death if she entered the inner court without being first summoned by the king.

The intensity continues to escalate, and every line of this story is a cliffhanger. Mordecai replied back with one of the most distinguished and legendary phrases found in God's Word. Follow along with me as we read it together: "Esther, don't think that just because you live in the king's palace you will be the only Jew to escape. If you keep quiet now, help and freedom for the Jews will come from another place. But you and your father's family will all die. And who knows, maybe you have been chosen to be the queen for such a time as this" (Esther 4:13–14 ERV).

Mordecai brought the truth in love, unashamedly pointing out that his trust is not in Esther but in the faithfulness of God. He reminded her that her own fate must also be found in the same thing. He then highlighted to Esther that going before the king, to save her people, might be the *real* reason why she became queen in the first place—her opportunity to live out the purpose that God had called her to.

Let's pause and contemplate this last expression for a moment. "For such a time as this." It is a poignant phrase that gives the waiting in our *going through* a whole new meaning and purpose.

Mordecai was essentially telling Esther that this moment she found herself in was an *opportunity*; it was pivotal that she had the courage and wisdom to seek God's understanding to accomplish the task. He never said it would be easy or comfortable for her, but it would require her sacrifice and obedience as she relied on God to walk her through. This same truth applies to us as well, even more so, I believe, in our waiting and our *going through.*

As we continue to follow Esther through her dilemma, let's keep our eyes wide open to what the Lord is teaching *us* through her story of waiting while *going through.* These words from Mordecai gripped Esther's heart and brought precision to her purpose in this challenging time for her people. She prepared herself to seek God wholeheartedly and to wait on His direction, knowing that His perspective was vital for what was to come.

After days of prayer and fasting, giving up all food and drink for three whole days while seeking the Lord, Esther went before the king *without* being summoned (Esther 5). She *boldly* defied the law in order to make her request. And believe it or not, the king permitted her to do so, stretching out his golden scepter in approval and offering her anything she wanted, "even if it is half the kingdom!" (Esther 5:3 NLT). However, instead of pleading for her people with emotion and desperation, she *waited*. It appears that she knew the timing wasn't quite right. God was clearly giving her the wisdom to bide time. Alternatively, she kindly invited the king to dinner.

King Xerxes accepted her invitation and showed up to Queen Esther's banquet, which seems to have been the next *perfect* opportunity for her to seek his help for her people. The king, once again, was willing to give Esther whatever it was she wanted, but again, she speaks nothing of the crisis of her people; instead, she *waited*, holding tightly to the Lord's leading and timing. She then invited the king and Haman to *another* dinner.

Before this next dinner, there were things taking place behind the scenes that you *must* know about. I believe it will give you understanding about her waiting, as it has for me. Continue adventuring though Esther 5:9–14 and Esther 6:1–14 to discover these wild, thought-provoking events.

As you complete your reading, are you seeing the *why* behind God leading Esther to *wait*? It's important to point out, these weren't activities Esther knew about. She had no idea about Haman's seventy-five-foot pole or the king's trouble sleeping. She just simply *trusted* God and *waited* for His timing to share the need with the king, while God moved in the details behind the scenes.

The day of the second dinner party came (Esther 7), and King Xerxes and Haman arrive. It was one more strategic opportunity for Esther to bring the predicament of her people to the king's attention. *But will she?!* The king once again was willing to give her whatever she wanted. And it appeared that this time, the timing was *finally* right. The waiting was over, and the Lord led Esther to share the quandary with the king. You'll have to read the rest of Esther's story to get all the remarkable intricate aspects of how God worked out the details in her waiting. The outcome will amaze you!

It's not specifically explained why Esther waited to speak to the king, but her story gives us glimpses as to the possibilities occurring backstage. Esther's *going through* did not provide her understanding like it does for us as we read her story. She was clueless as to the *why* behind her waiting, but it did not seem to matter to her. She simply sought God with all her heart, chose to trust Him, while waiting with hope *in Him*. Her obedience reveals she did what He led her to do, and because of that, she saw God's glory and goodness not only as a result of waiting but *in* the waiting as well. Her focus was fixed on the hope and confidence of God's divinity while she waited patiently on Him. Her heart was attuned to God alone and His specific leading. No reaction, just God-authorized responsiveness. This communicates to us the secret and the mystery of waiting. "For such a time as this." As He did with Esther, God moves in the details behind the scenes as we wait with hope and trust in Him alone.

Reflection Questions:

As you are *going through,* what have you been waiting for? Be honest; this is just between you and God.

Waiting can bring out the ugly in all of us, causing us to react only with our feelings and logic, instead of gaining understanding from God's perspective. Waiting can become frustrating when we're seeking a solution or a resolution on our own. Esther shows us the wise approach in the waiting: to pray and fast. To seek the Lord wholeheartedly while giving up our luxuries to do so. Fasting has a way of removing the *us* in our waiting and emphasizing our need of *Him*. Are you willing to seek the Lord as Esther did? If so, as you do, journal the words and direction God gives you as you seek Him with all of your heart during your waiting.

____

____

____

____

____

____

____

____

What does Esther's story teach you about what God is up to behind the scenes in the waiting of your *going through*?

God's Word brings us encouragement in our waiting. Take some time to write these verses down and meditate on what they're saying to you: Isaiah 40:31; Psalm 27:13–14; Lamentations 3:25–26; Micah 7:7; Psalm 130:5; Psalm 33:20–22.

As you wait, I want to inspire you to take each day to worship the Lord. There are two songs that I have on repeat that keep my heart tuned to Him: "Take Courage" by Kristene DiMarco and "Wait on You" by Elevation Worship and Maverick City Music. As you listen to these medleys, write down what the lyrics speak to you.

____

____

____

____

____

____

____

____

____

____

Going through will stir up our flesh in our seasons of waiting. But choosing to wait with hope in the Lord will always make the wait worthwhile. Choose today to trust Him wholeheartedly and obey His every instruction. For such a time as this, *you* can be encouraged. God is up to something behind the scenes, working out details you know nothing about. He intends to strengthen you to soar, bringing out the most beautiful conclusion in your waiting while you are *going through* with Him leading you.

Trust in and rely confidently on the LORD with all your heart and do not rely on your own insight or understanding. In all your ways know and acknowledge and recognize Him, and He will make your paths straight and smooth [removing obstacles that block your way].

(Proverbs 3:5–6 AMP)

CHAPTER 4

Broken

I was *finally* given the clear to go home, but not yet trusted to drive. The wife seat-belted herself into the driver's seat of my gray Topaz, while I sat shotgun in the passenger seat. I cried and trembled the whole way home, repeating to myself, under my breath, "Please don't die, Dad. Please don't die." Sobbing through *every* plea.

My eyes were swollen from the persistent crying and lack of sleep, but the sun had finally risen and was shining brightly, clearing out the fearsome fog and the thick darkness on our drive back. It was a refreshing sight, even as I shook with uncertainty not knowing if my dad would still be breathing when I arrived.

I could hardly sit still as the car approached the entrance of our property. While the car was still in motion, I was ready to jump out the door and run full speed ahead. The ambulance was there with several police cars parked all around our property. The sirens flashed while the authorities walked the land.

I grabbed the latch of the car door and swung it open. I couldn't sit any longer. The wife parked my car at least forty feet from my house to keep us back from all the commotion. She yearned for me to wait until we received the proper clearance to go into the house, but her desire and begging couldn't stop me. It was impossible. I was done waiting. I had to see my dad, mom, and sister *now*. I had to know they were okay.

I sprinted as if I were in a seventy-five-yard dash, arriving to my front door out of breath and parched. The police tried to question me at the entrance of my home, wondering who I was and why I was there, but I simply stated with a matter-of-fact tone in my voice, "I live here. I'm going in."

I made my way through the front entrance, and my eyes scanned our home looking for my mom as I cried out, "Mom! Where are you?" She met me in the living room with a loving embrace and a relieved look on her face. She was calm and collected, and I could see the presence of God was holding her together.

"How's Dad? Is he okay?! Is he still . . . alive?!" The questions fell out of my mouth like a two-hundred-pound brick I had been carrying for hours, while my eyes swelled from the overflow of tears bursting out. I shuttered to think what her answer could be. She assured me that he was still alive and that the first responders were with him, taking care of him. I couldn't help but bombard her with inquiries that had been boggling my mind all morning. "Who did this?! Who shot Dad? Why would they do this?" My interrogation didn't seem to overwhelm her as her face saddened with uncertainty; she simply responded with, "I don't know, honey."

As we waited for the paramedics to carry my dad down from his upstairs bedroom, my mom began to share *her* experience with me from that morning. We stood in the living room, at the side of the stair railing, while police scattered around us. They were no distraction to me, however, as I listened attentively to my mom as she began to unveil *her* view of that morning.

"He had a ski mask on." She commenced to describe the intruder's appearance along with the sights she recalled from that morning. *A ski mask?!* I thought. Immediately that told me that we must *know* this trespasser. *Why else would he be wearing a ski mask?!*

My mom described in detail that their bedroom light went on early that morning, but her eyes didn't open until she heard my dad speak. She then opened her eyes to see a man next to their bed, standing about three feet from her, on her left side. He was a holding a shotgun pointed directly at them.

The gunman's attire included a black ski mask with only openings for the eyes. He had a white shirt on with a tan vest. He was a bigger guy. She thought his shirt looked blousy or dressy in the sleeves, like a men's dress shirt. She thought it looked like he was outfitted to attend church, although accessorized with a hunting vest over his shirt, as if he was on a quest to kill.

She continued to explain the scene in further detail. As my dad spoke in a loud whisper, "Oh no!" the right side of his body slightly leaned upward toward the left where the gunman stood. His right arm stretched outward toward the intruder, while his right hand, palm facing out, gestured a hand signal that communicated, "Stop!" My dad was trying to create a barrier against the shot directed at both of my parents. My dad's left arm was wrapped tightly under my mom's body as she lay supine.

My mom closed her eyes immediately once she saw the gun pointing at them. She couldn't bear to watch what was about to take place. Just then she heard one shot ring out. The sound echoed through her ears while fear gripped her mind. The first shot had hit my father, and she knew the next gunshot was for her. Her thoughts began to wander, worrying about my little sister, Leah, and me being left without parents and wondering if the gunman planned to take *us* out next. She even wondered, even in those few seconds, whether the bullet would be painful if he pulled the trigger on her.

My mom sensed a long pause as her eyes squeezed tightly in despair, waiting for the next bullet to rush from the gun's chamber to hit her. When she finally opened her eyes—the time seemed to linger—she saw that the gunman was gone. She looked over at my dad who was thrashing and crying out in pain as he bled out all over their bedsheets.

As a nurse, my mom was able to explain to me in detail that the gunman had shot my dad point-blank in the chest. Later we discovered that the impact of the slug from a twelve-gauge shotgun, as it hit my dad's chest meticulously, it left a three-inch hole in his chest. The one ounce of lead missed his heart only by three quarters of an inch, but the blow collapsed his right lung and caused his colon to rupture, also breaking off ribs as it ripped through his body.

After I left to get help, my mom sent Leah to hold towels over my dad's two gaping holes: one in his chest, the entrance of the slug, and the other on his right side, about eight inches under his armpit, where the slug exited his body. The pressure would keep him from losing too much blood and going into hypovolemic shock.

My heart sank for both my mom and Leah, as I listened with fixed attention to my mom's retelling of events. The idea of my little sister attending to my dad's bleeding body caused a mix of emotion in me; my heart grieved at the thought but also swelled with amazement at her bravery. I had only glanced at my dad that morning in his excruciating condition, and it was torturous to see. I couldn't imagine watching my dad continue to bleed before me while he thrashed in agony and discomfort.

As Leah sat with my dying father, she cried out as fast as her tongue could express, "Jesus! Jesus! Jesus! Jesus!" She said His name in desperation as she stared out the bedroom window, waiting expectancy for an ambulance to arrive and save the day. Leah described later to me, in detail, the unforgettable scene of caring for my dad in those moments.

As she tried to hold the towels over his wounds, my dad would call out God's name in a long, low, miserable groan. "I'm dying! I'm dying!" my dad's voice shrieked repetitively. Every sound grew more faint with every second, and his words were slowly drowned out by his deep anguish.

"I need you, Daddy!" my little sister cried, shaky but strong, even demanding, as my dad began to say his good-byes to her. She begged and bartered with him for his life: "I need you more now than ever before! You can't leave me now!" Future thoughts without him in her life quickly flashed through my sister's mind, haunting and gripping her heart with agony. As she implored him to hang on, he rolled and thrashed on the queen-size bed, blood and fluid spilling out of him all the more.

Leah begged him to stop rolling as she tried to comfort him with sincere words, hoping to bring him peace in his pain. "God is here, Daddy. He's here with you right now." The smell of gunfire filled the room as Leah trembled with shaking hands, trying to hold the blood-soaked towels over our dad's squirming body as tightly as she could.

Just then, my dad began to speak his last and most significant words with the very little breath he had left inside him. He told my little sister, "Serve Jesus! Serve Jesus! I love you! Serve Jesus!" His words slowly began to turn into soft and unusual groans—murmurs that sounded like death settling in. It was a sound Leah had never heard nor will ever forget as she answered him, "I know, Daddy, I know."

Leah and I were very close growing up; she was not only my little sister but also a best friend to me through our awkward teenage years. So, as my mom described Leah's actions to me, I felt overwhelming appreciation for her. I was awe inspired by her bravery and her strength to be there with my dad, fully engaged in the care that he needed, as she spoke authentic truth to him in his suffering.

I began to tear up *yet again* as I listened to my mom's words. She had no answers or understanding as to *why* this had happened, but I felt relief and gratitude knowing she and Leah were safe and my dad was still breathing, at least at that moment. Just then, we began to hear movements from the upstairs bedroom.

Four men, uniformed as first responders, shuffled out the bedroom door, carrying a cot. I knew my dad was on it, but I couldn't quite see him because of the men surrounding him. Leah and I began jumping up and down steadily at the bottom of the stairs with hope infusing every leap, shouting, "We love you, Daddy! We love you!" Our cries were petitions to him, asking him to hold on and stay alive; we desperately needed him in our lives.

As the men with the makeshift bed descended down the stairway, we could *finally* see my dad's face. An oxygen mask covered his mouth and nose, while his body was wrapped tightly in blankets. He had lost seven pints of blood that morning, but he never lost consciousness. And what we knew, as they carried my dad down the stairwell, was that my dad was broken from the gunshot that blasted through his body but so were we as a family.

The next thing we saw spoke profoundly to my sister, my mom, and me. My dad began to communicate with us through a hand gesture that brought us expectation and optimism; it spoke louder than words ever could. His eyes slightly opened, and his body lay still and restful; his thumb slowly began to rise up, while his fingers formed a fist, giving us the universal thumbs-up symbol, letting us know he was okay. Even in his grave condition, it communicated to us *hope*—exactly what we needed in that moment. It was a beautiful reminder to all three of us: we may be broken from this, but we're not beyond repair.

Going through has a way of breaking something in us that we never intended to allow. Whether it's our heart or a relationship or our will to survive. It could be our thinking, maybe our feelings, or a piece of us we never knew could break. It might be our trust, or our loyalty, or our desire even to try. Whatever it may be, *going through* has a way of sneaking in and shattering us, crumbling a part of who we are, leaving us broken, in need of repair.

My season of *going through* brought a brokenness that left me feeling like a pile of ashes, scattered in the wind, irreparable. Are you feeling the same way in your season of *going through*?! It took years for me to truly see the One who loved me in my brokenness, the One who was willing to mend the dispersed pieces and bring life to my shattered soul. I finally found God's willingness to do so in me through a simple yet profound psalm written by David, a man from God's Word.

Have you ever read David's story? You know David—the giant killer, the warrior, and the king of Israel! Most of us have heard his heroic accounts of fierce protection over his sheep and have read his sweet and soothing poetry in the book of Psalms, but believe it or not, there's more to David's story than the exciting adventurous stuff.

Besides trampling wild animals and slaying bully-giants or singing worship songs in green pastures or writing poetry in the warm sun, he also felt the real struggle of *going through* and the realities of being broken himself. He faced tough challenges while making humungous mistakes. He dealt with rejection and went through trials that caused him to run and hide in fear. (Sound familiar?!) He experienced heartbreak and pain, sorrow, and defeat, and felt the damaging but healing discomfort of a contrite spirit. David too dealt with brokenness just like you and me.

There's so much to his story. I could never quite cover it all here, but I want to encourage you to take some time to get to know him and his special relationship with the Lord. His life story can be found in the books of 1 and 2 Samuel along with 1 Chronicles. But for now, will you join me in one of his special writings? Head to Psalm 51.

This chapter covers David's confession after he had made a massive and tragic mistake, one that not only hurt him but terribly impacted others around him. Nathan, a prophet, confronted David regarding his blunder (see 2 Samuel 11–12), and Psalm 51 is David's recognition and response regarding his *own* brokenness in the pain.

I love this chapter, but not for the reasons you may think. It's one of those chapters we can easily pass by and ignore, turning the page to a more uplifting psalm, one that will boost our spirits and fill us with joy. Psalm 51 is a prayer we may never *choose* to identify with, not wanting to apply its authentic and thought-provoking words to our own lives.

The writing in Psalm 51 doesn't make your heart jump up with excitement or give you goose bumps of goodness. There is no adventure in it or exhilaration to be found. Nope, none at all. Instead, it's David's real and raw emotions. His heart's desperate cry. His petition for God's repair.

This psalm displays the reality that Nathan's loving confrontation revealed God's view to David and now David knew, felt, and saw, beyond a shadow of a doubt, that he was in fact *broken*. However, his brokenness didn't cause God to run away or snub His nose in disgust. Nope. Instead, it did just the opposite. David's brokenness moved God's heart, drawing Him closer to David's brokenness so He could do what only God can do—bring redemption.

The sin of this fallen world brings brokenness, but Psalm 51 reminds us of God's goodness and restoration in our fragility. To me this chapter is a beautiful place for us to park and ponder the brokenness we face in our *going through*

seasons. Are you willing to do so with me?

As you read Psalm 51:1–4, what do you hear David saying? __________________

____

____

How would you describe his emotions? ______________________________

____

____

To me David sounds desperate, in need of repair; do you agree? As you continue

in verses 7–15, what is David asking God for? ________________________

____

____

____

____

____

____

In the end of Psalm 51, verses 16–19, David says something that changes everything, bringing light to his brokenness and hope to you and me as well. Read it with me: "You are not happy with any sacrifice. Otherwise, I would offer one to you. You are not pleased with burnt offerings. The sacrifice pleasing to God is a broken spirit. O God, you do not despise a broken and sorrowful heart" (Psalm 51:16–17 (GW).

David was a man after God's own heart. He was someone who regularly brought sacrifices to the temple to honor and worship the Lord. However, these two verses reveal his *new* understanding of sacrifice—a God-understanding of what true sacrifice really is.

It seems, as David continues in the psalm, he began to recognize the emptiness in living life without bringing his whole self, broken and all, to the Lord. He became comfortable with the secrets of his sins and the hypocrisy of his actions. He held the heavy burden of his hurts and continued to do things legalistically on his own, without allowing God to have every part of him.

David started to realize that his brokenness may be ugly to the world around him and may look weak among the strong. It may seem unpleasant to the thriving and frowned upon by the ones who seem to have it all together. It may be an annoyance and a nuisance to most people, but to God David's brokenness was beautiful. It was the perfect posture and position, a place of surrender, to be broken before and unto the Lord.

What the Lord really wanted from David was his *entire* heart. Every piece of it, whether it was punctured and battered, or broken in two, or shattered in little shards, lying helpless on the ground. It didn't matter to God what shape his heart was in as long as he was willing to give the entire thing to Him.

This is what the Lord wants from you too. He wants *all* of you. The places inside you like to hide. The damaged parts. The brittle and fragile pieces. The ugly portions. The rejection, the secrets, and the hot mess of hurts and pains you bury *deep* inside. The yuck that surfaces on your worst days. The stuff you stuff away to keep concealed from others. God wants it all, every last bit of it. It's His desire to be close to you, regardless of what shape you're in. He wants the *real* you, the messy you. The "you" you hide away. Why? The answer is clear throughout God's Word: because He loves you exactly as you are, all that you are, right where you are, right now, even in your brokenness. And nothing—and I mean nothing—can stop His love for you, not even your own brokenness (Romans 8:38–39).

Jesus understands brokenness better than anyone. His life is the greatest example we have because He actually *chose* to be broken for us. Jesus came to

Earth knowing He would take on *our* brokenness. He was despised and hated by those He came for (Isaiah 53:2–3). He carried the weight and heaviness of *our* sorrows (Isaiah 53:4). He was beaten and crushed so *we* could be healed (Isaiah 53:5). Even though we rejected Him, He still chose to do this for all mankind (Isaiah 53:6). He was willingly broken so that we could be made whole (1 Corinthians 11:23–26). Jesus paid this price for us in silence and without defense (Isaiah 53:8–9). I hope you truly come to realize: He understands *your* brokenness.

Jesus only requires *one* thing from you. Are you ready to hear it? If so, here it is. It's your willingness to give Him *all* (Mark 12:30). All of you for all of Him. It's an exchange: your yuck for His wholeness. And He won't take it, unless you give it. He won't stand in your way and force you to let go. He won't pry it away or pressure you to do it. He's a gentleman. His arms are wide open ready to receive, when *you're* ready. He will only take as you hand over yourself, brokenness and all. So what do you say?! Are you ready to lay it *all* down and hand *all of you* over to Him? Your brokenness is not beyond His repair.

Reflection Questions:

As you begin your reflection, I believe it's important to be real and raw with the Lord, as David was. The Lord desires intimacy with you, a closeness that allows you to be vulnerable and authentic with Him, just as He will be with you. Don't worry: your injured soul does not scare Him. He will not be run off by your messy thoughts or feelings. He is your refuge and safety, your help, the place you can run to (Psalm 46). Feel free to share openly and honestly with God on the lines below about the brokenness you've encountered in your *going through*.

____

____

____

____

____

____

____

____

As you share with the Lord, are you willing to give God *every* broken piece of you? Are you willing to lay down the hidden parts along with the deep, dark secrets? If so, let Him know, sharing *every* broken part of you with Him. Surrender it all at His feet.

____

____

____

____

____

____

____

____

____

____

____

David wrote another psalm that brings hope in our brokenness. Take some time to read Psalm 34. Study it and absorb every word. What is God's Word saying to you in this psalm?

____

____

____

____

____

____

____

____

____

____

____

____

Psalm 34:18 (NLT) says, "The LORD is close to the brokenhearted; he rescues those whose spirits are crushed." How does this verse bring you peace, rest, or hope in your *going through*? What remedy is God bringing you as you quit carrying your hurts and you hand *everything* over to Him?

____

____

____

____

____

____

____

____

____

____

There are a few songs that I love. The lyrics fill my spirit with hope in my brokenness. They are called "Broken Vessels (Amazing Grace)" by Hillsong Worship and "Pieces" by Bethel Music. I pray the lyrics do the same for you. As you listen, what is the Lord speaking to your broken heart?

Going through and brokenness go together, hand in hand, but being broken doesn't mean you're beyond repair. Jesus Himself was broken for you, in your place; He endured this because of His extravagant love for you. As you are willing to give Him all of you, He is willing to receive all of you, just as you are, brokenness and all—to bring you healing and restoration, mending every part of you, including your shattered soul.

> *[To] those in Zion who mourn. I will take away the ashes on their head, and I will give them a crown. I will take away their sadness, and I will give them the oil of happiness. I will take away their sorrow, and I will give them celebration clothes. He sent me to name them "Good Trees" and "The LORD's Wonderful Plant."*
>
> *(Isaiah 61:3 ERV)*

CHAPTER 5

Control

Leah and I clutched hands as we walked through the sliding glass doors of the hospital entrance together. The blandness of the walls brought us *no* comfort or certainty in our next steps. We had no words, just sobs and grief from the sights we had observed that morning. We clenched each other's hands with what strength we had left. We held our breath, unaware of what news we would receive from the medical staff as we walked down the hallway toward the next phase of unknowns.

As we entered the waiting room, the chairs and spaces were filled with people who loved my dad. They gathered around Leah and me with comforting hugs, tears, and expressions of "I love you." I cried harder and harder as I clasped my little sister's hand even tighter, knowing only she and my mom truly understood my grief. Their kind eyes and gentle embrace invited my emotions to release even while they continued to brew inside me.

After feeling alone and isolated all morning, it felt good to be surrounded by people. They came out of the woodwork, one group of individuals after another, with encouraging words and tears flowing from their eyes. It felt like a reunion, but under terrible circumstances, bringing us all together for just one man—my dad. People we knew from the past and those who were a part of our present-day lives flooded the hospital's bleak waiting room and stark hallways, bringing life to the atmosphere. The overwhelming support filled my spirit with joy, and it made sense why they were all there: my dad was a special man. He was loved by many.

My dad was one of those people who said hello to everyone. He knew no stranger. He greeted everyone he saw on the street and had conversations with random people in stores and public places. In fact, my entire childhood I believed that these people were friends of my father, people he knew, people he was affiliated with.

I remember one day I finally understood the truth about all my dad's so-called friends. I believe I was in the sixth grade at the time. As my dad and I wrapped up lunch together, we walked the streets of downtown Milford, Michigan. My dad did his usual thing and said his hellos to every passerby on the street. I remember looking up at him with curiosity and asking, "Who was that, Dad?" He smiled and responded, "I don't know, sweetie." I was puzzled, so I inquired further, "What about the person you said hi to before the last person, who was that?" He responded with the same answer: "I don't know, sweetie." He giggled as I looked at him perplexed. It was then the lightbulb of understanding went on in my head. "You mean, you've been saying hi to people you don't even know . . . all these years?!" I was completely flabbergasted as he responded nonchalantly with, "Yeah, I guess so." He laughed with a sweet smirk stretched across his face.

The saying, "More is caught than taught," couldn't be more true. As I grew up, I found myself doing the same exact thing as my dad, saying hello to every stranger I passed by and talking to random people in stores and public places, without realizing I was doing it. It wasn't until I was in my twenties when someone asked me that same exact question, "Who was that?" that reality hit me head-on and I laughed hysterically to myself. Shaking my head, I replied with my newfound insight: "I have no idea who that was! Oh my goodness, I've turned into my father."

As Leah and I continued to make our way through the hospital crowd, people directed us to a smaller surgical waiting room where immediate family sat with anticipation. Various voices shared the same update with us, that my dad was *still* in surgery, as friends ushered us through the mass of people. As we approached the condensed family waiting room, we were greeted by my mom and my siblings with a long embrace and more heavy tears.

My brother, Greg, was there, along with my sister, Jen, and her new husband, Joe. Their faces were distraught and in shock, their eyes red and swollen from crying. Jen began asking questions to gain understanding. She and Joe had begun their honeymoon the night before, after they had left their wedding celebration. I stared at Jen with heartbreak as she started asking the same frantic questions that had been going through *my* head. I noticed quickly she was still wearing her white high heels that had accompanied her bridal attire from her wedding the night before. My stomach ached to think that *this* was the start of her happily-ever-after marriage—a tragic event filled with sorrow and many unknowns.

The same question kept running through my mind and finally spewed from my mouth: "Who would do this?!" We talked as a family, waiting with uncertainty as my dad's life hung in the balance; we tried to make sense of this crazy, unbelievable, and horrifying situation. "Dad will know! He's got to know!" I blurted out. This was the only hope I could cling to; I needed my dad to come through this alive so he could reveal who he believed the perpetrator was.

As a pastor, my dad met with all sorts of people from various walks of life. He was committed to the Gospel of Jesus Christ and sharing God's love and goodness with everyone, and I mean *everyone*. Just as he confidently said hello to every stranger on the street, he also boldly told random people how much Jesus loved them. That was my dad; that was who he was. A man who reflected God's love to the world around him.

My dad counseled people daily. Listening and praying with couples dealing with marital problems, people with identity issues, individuals struggling mentally, emotionally, physically, and spiritually. He loved and helped people who had lost loved ones, who battled substance abuse issues, and who had once been imprisoned. He prayed for the sick, he encouraged the discouraged, and he shared truth with the lost. His door was *always* open, willing to point *any* hurting soul to the One who saved *his* soul.

We all agreed as a family: the gunman could be someone he'd counseled or tried to help or even someone from the past. *If he comes out of this,* I thought to myself, *we can get the answers we all want and the justice we all need so we can return to normal.* We prayed together as a family, huddled in that small room, hoping for my dad's life to be spared on the surgical bed as time ticked away slowly.

Just as the daylight had brought some hope that morning, the doctor who performed my dad's surgery walked into the quaint waiting room with a somewhat optimistic announcement. My dad had survived the twelve-gauge shotgun slug that blew swiftly through his body at close range, but now there were other concerns that endangered his life. After about eight hours of surgery, my dad was now in critical condition in the intensive care unit on a ventilator, heavily medicated through intravenous therapy. The medical staff wanted to keep a close watch for peritonitis, a contamination in the blood that could be life-threatening. Because of my dad's ruptured colon from the shotgun blast, there was a chance of infection that now threatened his life.

My mom was the only one allowed to see my dad at this time. The first twenty-four hours after surgery were crucial to his survival. He needed rest and a close watch and, most importantly, prayer. My exhausted family continued to wait with hope that my dad's life would, in fact, be restored as we made the ICU waiting room our new home.

My strength was depleted; my mind was a wreck. My emotions were unstable and my body fatigued as I made my provisional bed on the ICU waiting room floor, alongside my worn-out family members. We lay *restless* on the tile as the horror of that day finally seemed to come to a close. We tried to get the respite we all *desperately* needed, while the hospital sounds filled the adjacent hallway and illuminating lights shone brightly through the crack of the door. A police officer was dispatched outside the ICU entrance for my dad's protection, just in case the gunman came back with a vengeance.

As the room got quieter, I knew the others were starting to fall asleep, one by one, but my mind had no plans of following suit. My thoughts continued to race and rattle, trying to make sense of the sights and sounds I had experienced that morning. My mind quickly adapted to the pivotal need to stay alert to my surroundings so I wouldn't again miss a beat. I knew I needed to stay in control so I could stay well-informed of what was happening around me.

That first sleepless night on that hard-tiled hospital floor was just the beginning of my restlessness and striving to stay in control. I needed rest, but I felt as though rest just made me weak. I was not willing to surrender or submit to anyone or anything, including the *necessity* of sleep. My mind stayed constantly alert and on the go so I could be ready for anything. I relied fully on myself, not on God or anyone else, for that matter. I was also committed to finding answers on my own. I wanted justice and I wanted it *now*, and I believed if I stayed attentive and watchful, I would find it.

I felt as though I had to keep myself and everything in control in order to protect myself and my family from future pain. This way of thinking turned me into a control freak, believing if I could regulate my surroundings, then none of us would have to endure this pain any longer. Being in control was my new coping mechanism, and over time it began to deteriorate my health and destroy my faith with each passing day.

Are you feeling this way in your *going through*? It's not like we mean to be controlling, right?! It's all part of our human nature, of course. But when we're *going through* something painful and difficult, it will oftentimes provoke a need in us to control something or someone, in order to guard ourselves and protect us from further heartache and more headache. Have you noticed this about yourself?

It's a sneaky fleshly feeling of wanting to take over and have full reign, leaving God out of the equation, because in our heart (let's be honest!) we're not quite sure He can handle it. The root of it is pride, and we're not fully convinced He'll bring the answers we want, or the comfort we need, or the justice we feel we deserve. So we step in and do *our* thing, *our* way.

Don't worry, we're not the *only* ones with control issues. There are others just like us, I promise. And the truth is, the more honest and real we are with ourselves, the quicker we'll be able to find freedom from it.

There are people scattered about, even in the Bible, with the same sort of control problem. The good news is, Jesus seems to have a compassionate heart for us control freaks. He even likes to invite people like us to follow Him, revealing His heart for our kind.

Before we move on, it's probably a good time to pause and think about any control issues you've discovered about yourself in your season of *going through*. I feel as though the best way to help you see what it is you try to control is to have you take a few moments and answer the following questions. As you do, please answer with honesty and sincerity. I believe you will find some much-needed understanding about yourself and your needs. Are you ready? Here it goes.

What needs to happen or be in place in order for you to have a good day?

____

____

____

____

____

____

____

What stands out to you that you try to control in order to have a good day?

____

____

____

____

____

As you reflect on what you wrote above, what are the things you *can't* control?

____

____

____

____

What are the things you *can* control?

____

____

____

____

Is it becoming more clear to you as you ponder and write?! Your answers to these questions reflect your rule and reign over what you constitute as making the day good or bad. And the truth is, a day shouldn't be considered good just because of your level of control during that day. Ouch! I know that hurts, because I've had to learn it too. But it's one more step in the right direction. So, let's break it down: What is it really? What do you try to control in order to have a day that you consider good? Is it your circumstances, people, your schedule, the traffic . . . what is it *really*?

____

____

____

____

____

____

____

____

____

As we continue, please know that your honesty and self-reflection bring you closer to healing and breakthrough. It brings us nearer to surrender and letting go when we allow God to have His place in our lives, especially in our *going through* seasons. Once you recognize the areas you try to control, you may begin to recognize how it deteriorates your health and destroys your faith, just like it did mine.

How is your need to control infecting and poisoning certain areas of your life?

____

____

____

____

____

____

____

____

____

Are your attempts to control doing any good? ___________ If so, how? If not, why not?

____

____

____

____

____

____

____

____

____

____

____

____

As you ponder your responses, let's jump into God's Word to read about one of my favorite control freaks whom Jesus loved and adored and accepted (phew!). His life has been an encouragement and a relief to me; I hope it will be to you as well. His name and actions can be found throughout the New Testament; his personality traits can be seen clearly in various stories and his accounts found in many books, including the Gospels and the book of Acts.

This man was Simon Peter, a strong-willed, outspoken, passionate, impulsive, and sometimes harsh individual. He was considered a pillar of the church and one of Jesus's first followers and closest friends. We can see his boldness and leadership qualities shine brightly while his failings and flaws flow consistently. However, Jesus *still* chose Peter, imperfections, controlling issues, and all, while He also patiently and gently shaped him into the person, follower, and leader He called him to be, regardless of his control-freak ways (Thank You, Jesus!).

Meet me in John 18; we'll start there. Jesus and His followers entered a grove of olive trees as we begin this chapter. It had been about three years since these men began following Jesus. They had shadowed Him closely, watching His every move, including raising the dead, healing the sick, teaching the truth to the lost, and sharing hope with the hurting. They had left *everything* to learn and understand Jesus firsthand as He walked on water, multiplied food, provided wine out of water at a wedding, and taught them how to pray in pivotal moments of their ministry together. Jesus was their Mr. Miyagi, and they were His Daniel-son, the Teacher and His students.

Simon Peter himself had experienced personal miracles and encounters with Jesus in those three years: Jesus healed his mother-in-law; they had a little water walking on the Sea of Galilee together; Jesus invited him to experience God's glory on Mount Tabor; and He even gave Simon his added name, Peter, meaning rock.

And here now we see them all together, Rabbi and pupils, at the olive grove. The disciples followed Jesus to the place where Roman soldiers, temple guards, leading priests and Pharisees equipped with torches, lanterns, and weapons met them. And they showed up for one thing: to arrest the disciples' best friend, their Lord and Master, Jesus Christ, in this olive orchard.

Jesus was well aware of what was going to happen to Him. He willingly surrendered Himself, and you would think at this point Simon Peter would've understood what was going to happen as well. All six chapters prior to this moment, Jesus spent predicting, explaining, teaching, and telling His disciples what was to come, but for some strange reason, in this moment, they didn't seem to get it. Well, at least Peter didn't, and we can see this firsthand by his actions.

The tensions were high as the slew of soldiers surrounded them. They could all see Judas, supposedly one of *them*, leading the pack of arrestors, ready to take Jesus, dead or alive. With his personality, Peter couldn't help but react; he was imprudent and zealous, but who could blame him?! Peter knew they were there for the One he called his Teacher, Rabbi, and Lord, so he did what Peter always did: he took control and reacted. Out of fear and desperation, Peter rose up with a show of power and protection, with hopes to save Jesus and to defend them all. The "hero" inside him ascended to the occasion. The righteous anger that fueled Peter's actions as he watched the betrayer, their so-called friend Judas, stand before them. And then it happened. Peter did a thing. He tried to take control of something that was completely out of his control. As we read on, we can see his next move.

John 18:10 (ERV) provides a clear view of the scene: "Simon Peter had a sword, which he pulled out. He struck the servant of the high priest and cut off his right ear." This was Peter's opportunity to fulfill his promise that he'd made to Jesus: to defend Him at all costs, even to the point of death (Matthew 26:35). Peter's pretty dramatic and seemed to believe he had to prove himself to Jesus, to show his loyalty and strength and possibly even his value. However, Peter's warrior-like actions were not a shining display of courage. His need to control the situation looked more like a fallout than a victory. He cut the ear off of a *servant*; he didn't go swords-a-blazing on a *Roman soldier*.

Peter's reaction revealed his weakness; his need to rule revealed his lack. It was not only detrimental to his health (and those around him) but also devastating to his faith. Everything the Lord had been teaching him up to this point seemed to go out the window with one slice of an ear! Peter wasn't willing to surrender to God's will and trust the path Jesus had chosen to take for Peter and for us.

Jesus quickly reprimanded Peter as He reminded Peter once again of the route He must take. "Put your sword back in its place! I must drink from the cup the Father has given me" (John 18:11 ERV). In other words, "Peter, let go of trying to control what scares you so I can fulfill what I was called to do—bring you freedom from your need to control!"

As the chapter continues, you can see it all goes downhill for Peter from there. While Jesus was questioned by the authorities, Peter was in hiding and lied about knowing Jesus—not once, not twice, but *three whole times*! And after the rooster crowed for the last time, after Peter's third lie, we don't hear from him again until a few chapters later.

Now head on over to John 21. Go ahead and read it on your own. What do you find interesting? How do the words of Jesus penetrate your heart? This chapter reflects the resurrected Jesus, the One who has completed His mission for you, me, and even Peter.

Jesus appeared to His friends once again, including a flawed and failed Peter from John 18. And, interestingly enough, Jesus appeared to them at a familiar and comfortable place where Peter was known to spend a lot of time—the Sea of Galilee—a second home to Peter, a place where he fished often, and the same location Jesus met and called Peter to follow Him. It was also the same body of water that Jesus and Peter walked on together.

That sea had *history* for Peter and Jesus. The recollections, memories, and ease surrounded Peter in that place, and it's quite possible that was what brought Peter back to that body of water this particular day (John 21:3). Well, third time's the charm, they say. And this third meeting Jesus had with Peter, in *this* place, speaks volumes about the character of Jesus. Jesus *will* meet with us; He will encounter us exactly where we are, even in the places and things we run to that bring us comfort. He is tenacious and intentional in pursuing us wherever we go.

The closing conversation in John 21 between Jesus and Simon Peter speaks deeply to my soul. Jesus reinstated Peter with three repetitive loving but confrontational questions, reminding and reiterating Peter of his *real* role, the one that God had called him to. Amazingly, Jesus never pointed out what Peter had done wrong the days before; there's no pointing fingers or bringing up his failures and faults. Instead, Jesus gave Peter insight based on what was *His*, not what was Peter's. This reveals God's sovereignty in the midst of Peter's controlling nature.

Jesus showed His mercy and forgiveness wrapped in *real* love, a response that said He didn't need Peter's grip on things but instead sought a heart willing to trust and obey. Jesus instructed Peter to feed His sheep, implying a new position for Peter: to care for what was in God's hands, not in Peter's hands. However, it would require Peter to fully surrender to what God led him to do. Peter could no longer rule and reign *his* way, but instead he had to rest and rely on *God's* way.

After this encounter with Christ, we find a new Peter. One who appeared to be free from doing *his* thing, *his* way. One who no longer had to react impulsively and respond imprudently. Peter went from cutting off an ear with a sword (John 18:10) to piercing hearts with God's truth (Acts 2:37). No denying Christ any longer or bossing people around. Nope. Peter was changed. His surrender put control back in the hands of the One to whom it belonged. Peter's story encourages me to do the same: to release my grasp on life and allow God's will to catch what I let go of.

How about you? Are you willing to let go and trust the One who is really in control? It will require vulnerability and complete yielding. It will be challenging and unsettling at times. It requires a step of faith *daily* to relinquish the control our flesh has held on to for so long. However, as we choose to lay it all down and hand over the reins to Him, we will discover the same freedom Peter experienced firsthand as he wrote personally about it in 1 Peter 5:7 (NLT), "Give all your worries and cares to God, for he cares about you."

Reflection Questions:

You've already taken the time to write down what you've been trying to control.

Now it's time to talk to the Lord about *relinquishing* that control. Take a few

minutes to write about your willingness to do so.

____

____

____

____

____

____

____

____

____

____

____

As you write about your willingness to let go of the reins, how is your heart and

soul beginning to feel free as you release the clenching grip you once held?

As when breaking any bad habit, we must start with one day at a time. This is also the first step in releasing control. I want to encourage you to take each day and lay down before the Lord the people or situations you've been trying to control. There are many ways to do this. You can speak to God out loud—"I give you this person or situation"—or write down what it is you want to release and surrender to God in prayer. It may be a list of areas in your life you hang up in a familiar place so you can read it and reiterate what you're handing over to Him. You may want to journal to the Lord each day, prayerfully surrendering each person or situation with intentionality. Whatever way you choose to release and relinquish on purpose, take time to write, on the lines below, about how it's impacting you.

____

____

____

____

____

____

____

What is taking place as you choose to lay your need for control at the feet of Jesus? Write about the journey: the good, the bad, and the ugly. What kind of freedom are you feeling? What wisdom and insight is the Lord instilling in you?

As you close out this chapter, take some time to listen to this beautiful song of surrender: "Letting Go" sung by Steffany Gretzinger. What are the lyrics speaking to you? How does letting go place you in God's hands? Write your answers below. Another one of my favorite jams to listen to regularly is "Everything Is Yours" by Maverick City Music. It is a constant reminder that it's all His anyway. We can trust His sovereignty and our lives surrendered to Him. There is freedom and healing in this awareness.

____

____

____

____

____

____

____

____

____

Going through invokes a need to take control, grasping the reins with our fear intertwined with our pride. Our control sometimes causes us to join causes that Christ never called us to. We use it as a way to protect and guard ourselves with our own human strength, which results in destroying our health and devastating our faith. It turns us into control freaks, a toxic position and a draining role that the Lord *never* called us to. Choose instead to relinquish all your control. You have a Father in heaven who cares more for you than you can possibly imagine. His unconditional love paid the price for you to let go and fully trust in Him. He is sovereign and in control so you don't have to be. Let go and fall into Him.

Give all your worries and cares to God, for he cares about you.

(1 Peter 5:7 NLT)

CHAPTER 6

Fill the Void

After twenty-four hours, my sisters and I were *finally* given the approval to see our father. The visit came with warnings from doctors and even church members reminding us that our dad's appearance may frighten us. "He's not going to look like himself. There's going to be tubes, lots of them. He will be connected to machines that beep and alarm!" They shared the forewarnings with compassion to prepare our fragile minds. I was grateful. Their cautionary insight brought reality to the unrealistic vision of my dad that I had conjured up in my head.

We walked through the darkened and quiet ICU. This section of the hospital seemed like a planet of its own. The silence was painful and dreadful, despite the subtle but constant, annoying beeps coming from each room that encircled the nurse's station. The nurse on duty walked us toward our dad's chamber. I took a slow, deep breath to prepare my emotions for the obscured view I was warned about concerning my father's appearance.

The warnings did in fact prepare us. My dad was encapsulated by machines with multiple tubes that seemed to connect to every inch of his body, providing a life-giving antidote or removing something that didn't belong. Each one of us teared up at the sight because this was not a picture of who our dad really was. He was a man full of life, on the go, always bouncing around, moving about with a smile stretched across his face ear to ear, with intentional joy oozing out of him. Our hearts broke to see him broken like this.

We immediately began to tell him how much we loved him while his pale, swollen body shook vigorously from the pain medication that pumped through his veins. My dad's eyes were closed tightly, his face puffy from trauma, and the sound of the ventilator kept time as it pumped oxygen into his lungs. He nodded as if he could hear us, while he twitched and quivered; tears streamed from the corners of his eyes, down his cheeks.

We began to sing together as sisters, in unison, just like we did when we were little. We held his hands securely while we sang the hymn "Oh, How I Love Jesus." The lyrics poured from our shaky vocal chords between sobs of sadness, filling us with memories of our childhood. We sang out every word precisely from several different melodies.

As kids, my sisters and I would put worship records on and walk circles around our living room for hours. Saturday afternoons we took over the record player and blasted tunes. We sang our hearts out to Jesus. We would harmonize and take turns having solos as we worshipped the Lord to the cranked-up sounds on the stereo of Psalty the Singing Songbook, Don Francisco, Amy Grant, Harvest, and Keith Green. We would occasionally catch our parents peeking in at us from around the corner, with tear-filled eyes. As a child, I didn't understand their tears; I thought maybe they were just happy tears because we weren't fighting with one another, but now as a mom, I completely get it. Seeing your children *choose* to worship the Lord without instruction, of their own accord, might be one of the most beautiful sights to witness as a parent.

With each passing day, my dad continued to improve. The prayers that people were praying around the nation were bringing hope to our simple, unknown family of six from our small suburban town in Michigan. And within a week my dad was taken off the ventilator and moved to a regular room in the main hospital. Unable to fully speak because of being on the ventilator for five days, my dad communicated through paper and pen.

It was finally time to get the answers we desperately needed. My dad was healing rather quickly and was fully conscious and aware. His insight could give us understanding as to who did this to him and perhaps why.

The question was finally asked as my dad lay slightly upright in the hospital bed, the tray table pulled closely to his chest. His pen gripped securely in his right hand, the paper lay before him. He scribbled words as his eyes swelled with tears. I watched with anticipation for an answer that would solve the mystery that almost took out his life and disrupted our family in such a painful and traumatizing manner.

My mom stood next to him preparing to recite his jotted writing. Her face revealed his scrawled answer before she even said a word. "He doesn't know who it was," she proclaimed. It was disheartening to hear, but it just caused our family to rally together more intently. However, our investigation continued as we sat in my dad's hospital room that day; our family discussed people and possible motives, while my dad wrote as quickly as he could to bring his insight and understanding to the conversation.

My heart sank as I began to realize the mystery surrounding the premeditated murder of my dad. My hope continued to spiral downward with no firm answers or any understanding. The questions that bombarded my thoughts overwhelmed my mind and sickened my stomach. Fear gripped me with the uncertainty of the *who*, the *why*, or the *what's next*.

My attention turned to the police for justice. I met with them constantly, as if I had become one of them, going over details and having discussions with detectives regarding the sights, sounds, suspects, and motives of the crime. While the inquisition grew more intense, our local police department partnered with more experienced detectives from surrounding cities who were skilled in calculated homicides; they began digging deeper, questioning family members, church attendees, and past acquaintances.

My mind was turned on continuously, going and going, searching and searching, for the sake of justice, of course. I invested myself in the cause because I needed closure, not only for the sake of my dad and my family but also for the sake of my own sanity. I felt as if I was putting together a ten-thousand-piece jigsaw puzzle, day in and day out, trying to connect the dots by putting each fragment and portion in its place to make sense of the real-life mysterious tragedy that had happened in my house.

During my dad's recovery in the hospital, close friends accompanied my mom, sister, and me back to our home, during the daylight hours, so we could gather belongings we needed while we slept at the hospital. It was an eerie feeling to be going back for the simple things, like a change of clothes or a new pair of contacts. The haunting memories from that morning made me jump at my own shadow; fear forced me to need someone to walk me through each room. It was frustrating to feel so insecure and violated in the place where I should feel the safest. The emptiness I felt was painful. The unrest, the uncertainty, and the turbulence stirred me up and drained me dry.

While my dad recuperated and our family resided at the hospital during his next phase of recovery, church friends prepared our home for our return: cleaning blood stains from the carpet, hanging curtains to provide privacy, installing an alarm system for protection. They knew we had encountered serious shock and overwhelming agony there as a family, so they did whatever they could to deliver hope, help, and wholeness for our return.

After ten days of healing from a twelve-gauge shotgun slug that had bombarded my dad's body and wreaked havoc in his chest cavity, my dad was discharged from the hospital: a recovery miraculous to every person who witnessed his recuperation. It was now time for our family to move back to the place where this had all begun, the place we used to call home. But we weren't quite ready to move back home just yet.

The police had a few people on their radar they were calling "persons of interest" in the case; however, the evidence was lacking and there were too many unknowns. One individual specifically, who seemed like the most likely assailant, was not willing to cooperate with the investigation, causing more frustration and time to lag. The police knew that each passing day brought them further from solving the case, so our family chose to stay hidden in a home of close family friends for about a week or two so we could decide on our next steps.

During this time of solitude, our family discussed what those next steps should be—a topic I've come to realize you never really discuss unless there's been heartache and you're forced to have to make some life-altering decisions. Since the criminal was still at large, the threat of another attack seemed imminent. Police, along with close friends and family, asked us the same question over the weeks following this event: "Are you going to move away and change your names?" This question caused us to come together and discuss whether or not we would. We knew the gunman had a death wish for my dad, and if he hadn't accomplished it with the last attack, what would stop him from another attempt?

My dad left the decision of whether or not to stay up to my mom. My mom's response was as fierce as her feisty and profound faith. She declared with certainty, "The enemy would want us to run, but God is with us. He gave us our home, and we're going back to it. We will not move away and live the rest of our lives running in fear." And just like that, we moved back home.

The weeks turned into months, and I tried to cope with my new lease on life once we returned home. Every time the sun went down, turmoil set in, adrenaline pumped through my veins, and anxiety clutched my emotions. The daylight brought me a sense of rest and reassurance that we had made it through another night, but the evenings brought darkness that caused me to relive the trauma of that painful morning of October 27 . . . over and over and over again.

Church members took turns sleeping with a loaded weapon at the entrance of our home, ready to take out the intruder if he tried to return. Our house alarm was set each night as the evening sky welcomed the dusk; every exit door of our home was connected to the security system to bring us awareness of anyone who tried to enter. Our family gathered in the living room, sleeping on couches, reclining chairs, and the carpeted floors as we clutched our own weapons: a golf club, a fire extinguisher, and a baseball bat. The outside lights attached to our house shone brightly, encircling the outskirts of the exterior walls like Fort Knox. My new normal at home didn't feel so normal after all.

As we all began losing hope in the justice system, I began losing hope altogether. There were no answers coming about the case, and there was no one in custody for committing this crime. I was encouraged by people around me to start living again, to do the things I'd planned to do before this terrible event occurred. Time was marching on without my permission, and I was stuck waiting for answers that weren't coming and may never come.

I decided to take their advice to live again but found myself filling the void from the pain I felt instead. I didn't quite know *how* to start again; I was stuck, confined, and paralyzed by fear and uncertainty, which seemed to change everything about me. The PTSD burrowed a hefty hole inside me that began to hollow out the life I once had.

I felt dead inside, but also hot-wired with anxiety, stress, and suffering, triggered by this event that had taken full control over my identity. I turned to busyness, alcohol, a new job, making new friends, staying out and trying to drown out the ordeal and the sorrow that imprisoned my soul. I stuffed my emptiness with anything I could find. And as long as I kept going and moving, I believed I could continue to bury the pain, the anguish, and the grief deeper and deeper inside until maybe, just maybe, it would all just disappear.

Fill the void. That was my remedy, my antidote. The problem is—a void that great can't be filled with superficial fillers. I had an internal wound so deep, so dark, and so hollow, it was infecting everything in me and influencing everything about me. The unfulfilling fillers were dictating my friendships, my relationships, my choices, my decisions, my lifestyle, my character, and even my destiny.

Those close to me at the time began to see it clearly: I was a hot mess, to say the least, and I was quickly unraveling before their eyes. They decided to meet with me and confront my erratic choices and behaviors. However, their confrontation brought no hope or answers to take the place of my pain. They had nothing else to offer in its place. There was no remedy they could bring or peace they could provide to help me heal or cope. So without something to fill the gap, I stuck with what I knew, even if it was destroying who I was and who I was meant to be.

What about you? Are you trying to do the same thing, filling the void that the *going through* has burrowed dangerously deep inside you? The void is the chasm where pain has hollowed out your soul, the place where God's peace and joy, His strength and hope, are *meant* to reside. It's the gap we try to fill with superficial relationships, artificial fillers like substances and busyness, and unfulfilling identities, habitual habits, tasks, and agendas. And in order to keep the void *feeling* full, we find ourselves continuing with the same chaotic, erratic actions, because if we don't, God forbid, the hole grows larger and deeper, into an abyss of loneliness and loss. And we just can't handle the pain of that desolation.

Well, I'm here to tell you, there is something fulfilling, and I found it. *Someone* that fills the chasm greater than your fake fillers ever could. It's an antidote so great you will never, ever look anywhere else—ever again. *I promise.*

I finally found it after I came to the end of my rope, unable to sustain the striving, the doing, the filling and the going round and round in circles any longer. I was *done* living out the definition of insanity, doing the same thing and expecting a different result but never achieving it.

Are you done too? Are you weary and tired of trying to fill up your hollowed heart and empty soul with stuff that doesn't last? Are you exhausted from the sorrows that stole the life right out of you and left you with a gaping hole you wish would heal? If so, please keep reading. The goodness is found as we adventure further, and I can't wait for you to see it for yourself as we dig into God's Word together.

There's an unnamed woman I discovered in the Bible who showed me the One who could seal the gap. Her story is found in John 4:1–26. You might see yourself in her personality, just as I have seen myself. Let's turn there now and learn about her life story *together.*

As you read, you can probably see firsthand, this Samaritan woman was an outcast. She seemed to do things on her own, *her* way, plugging away at life, in her *own* strength, in her *own* timing. It's easy for us simply to read the words of her story, but I want to encourage you to step *into* her story—*her* situation and *her* sandals—so you can better understand *her* predicament. Engage your senses in the details. I believe, as you do, the Holy Spirit will reveal exactly what you need to fill the void you have been harboring.

This woman's nationality caused others to look down on her, while the ladies in her hometown wanted nothing to do with her. No coffee dates with real friends or encouraging words sharpening her soul. Her life seems to be a series of striving, searching, and looking for *something* or *someone* to fill the gap and quench her constant thirst.

She traveled to the well alone, each day, midday, when the sun was hot and uncomfortable. She seemed to be self-reliant, quick to speak with strangers, physically strong, yet hard-hearted from the burdens and letdowns of life. As she arrived at her usual spot around noon this specific day, she was greeted by a Jewish man, who seemed to be intentionally waiting for her. We know this man fondly as Jesus, the King of Heaven. However, she just saw a man, not the Son of God; He was no one special to her. His appearance, from her stance, probably reminded her of everything she was not, reminiscent of every man who had ever let her down.

Jesus did His usual thing, breaking cultural barriers and transcending legalistic laws. He acknowledged her and even talked to her, asking her for a drink of water from the well where they had met. She was surprised and shocked that He recognized her. However, more importantly, Jesus's response to her spilled the truth of why He had stopped to meet her there, personally, in the first place. He deliberately pointed out that if she only knew who He was, she'd be asking Him for the life-giving water that only He could bring. But she didn't seem to understand His comments. Instead, her sarcasm kicked in strong, revealing the countless times she'd had to defend herself, her need to give a fierce answer in response to every put-down and degrading comment she'd ever heard. Hurt people hurt people. And although she seemed to be looking for something to fill her void, she didn't seem to know *how* to receive what He was offering, and maybe that's because she'd never been offered anything of worth before this very moment.

The cool part is, Jesus didn't seem bothered or offended by her sarcasm or brashness; instead, He responded lovingly with weighty and to-the-point answers that He knew she needed in that very moment. Her void had been growing larger by the day, while her personal striving and relying on her own strength was exhausting her. Jesus told her, "Everyone who drinks this water will get thirsty again and again. Anyone who drinks the water I give will never thirst—not ever. The water I give will be an artesian spring within, gushing fountains of endless life" (John 4:13–14 MSG). It seems that this announcement from Jesus got her attention, and rather quickly; she was intrigued, though her curiosity was mixed with cynicism, and she seemed to want what He said He could give her.

Jesus then pushed the boundaries of cultural propriety even further as He encouraged her to get her husband and come back to the well with him. She responded openly and bluntly, letting Him know she didn't have a husband, but Jesus already knew that. This was *His* opportunity to reveal what He knew and what she didn't know. It was an open door for Jesus to speak supernaturally to her real story, the one she kept behind closed doors, with a guarded heart and a strong boarded-up exterior.

Jesus's response to her was priceless. John 4:18 (MSG) shares His words: "That's nicely put: 'I have no husband.' You've had five husbands, and the man you're living with now isn't even your husband. You spoke the truth there, sure enough."

Immediately she recognized that Jesus was someone special who may have the answers she'd been longing for. She started to ask questions that pertain to her spiritual stumbling blocks, the things that had frustrated her and discouraged her from seeking the One who could fill her empty soul. Their conversation continued as they discussed true worship, and Jesus answered her inquiries and alluded to what was coming and who was right in front of her. He lovingly confronted her self-reliant, void-filling lifestyle in order to bring her to a place of making a profound decision: preparing her to see Him as He is.

Just then, Jesus revealed the remedy, the antidote she'd long desired to quench her parched soul. A personal, close, authentic relationship with the One, the Christ, who dissipates the burden, the pain, the trauma, and the hurt. The Messiah who fills up chasms with an overflowing of His love and ridiculous goodness. John 4:21–26 describes His words beautifully; they were shining like a precious treasure personally, just for her, something that had been hidden from her sight up until now: "'I am he,' said Jesus. 'You don't have to wait any longer or look any further'" (John 4:26 MSG).

Finally, in *that* moment she could truly see Him for who He really was. She didn't have to look any further, no more striving or searching to fill the void. She dropped her water jar in amazement and ran back to her village to tell everyone about Him—the One who knew everything about her and everything she ever did. The One who knew her messy insides and guarded exterior. The One who chose to meet her purposefully where she was and faithfully wait until she arrived, offering her His thirst-quenching friendship with love and acceptance intertwined.

This interaction began a contagious chain reaction! If you continue to read the rest of the chapter, you can see for yourself the magnitude of this one simple conversation over water at a well, between a parched woman and the Well of Life! Jesus immediately prepared His disciples for what was to come, knowing there were other thirsty souls longing for His life-giving water, as the woman ran to town to share the good news with everyone she met. Jesus recycled her pain into purpose and made her His first missionary in that Samaritan village.

Many of the Samaritans from that village committed themselves to him because of the woman's witness: "He knew all about the things I did. He knows me inside and out!" They asked him to stay on, so Jesus stayed two days. A lot more people entrusted their lives to him when they heard what he had to say. They said to the woman, "We're no longer taking this on your say-so. We've heard it for ourselves and know it for sure. He's the Savior of the world!" (John 4:39–42 MSG)

I hope this glimpse of the Samaritan woman's story speaks deeply to your situation. I hope you see for yourself: Jesus is all you need, your fulfillment. He is the One with the living water that fulfills and satisfies more beautifully than any substance, activity, or attention you've been seeking. He is the One who replenishes and replaces your striving and doing and going about. Jesus is ready and willing to meet you exactly where you are. He is the One true fulfillment for the one empty soul. And only He satisfies.

As you walk through the following reflection questions, ponder honestly your fillers and the results that they bring. Are you willing to drop them at the feet of the One who abundantly refreshes? He is the One who wants to fill your empty chasms with His contagious, authentic, and zealous love. You won't be disappointed, I promise.

Reflection Questions:

It's time to get real with yourself and the Lord. What kind of faulty fillers have you been focused on to fill the empty gaps in your heart? Are you willing to drop them, like the Samaritan woman dropped her water jar, so you, too, can receive the only love that fully satisfies? Pour your heart out with your words, as you jot it all down below.

____

____

____

____

____

____

____

____

____

As you've identified the things you do to try to fill your wounds, what have been the results of your striving and doing in your own strength, in your own way? How is your way of doing things going against God's plans and who He made you to be?

____

____

____

____

____

____

____

____

____

____

____

The moment the woman at the well recognized Jesus as the One who could fill her soul to overflowing, her heart softened and she became completely transparent. She was free from her striving and self-sufficiency. Her authenticity was revealed as she proclaimed with no shame to everyone around town, "Come and see a man who told me everything I ever did . . ." (John 4:29 NLT). As you recognize Jesus as the same One who wants to fill *your* soul and free *you*, how does this soften your heart and cause you to be real and transparent with Him, the one you call your Messiah?

____

____

____

____

____

____

____

____

____

Take some time to search the following scriptures, reminding yourself of His life-giving love and fulfillment: Psalm 145:15–16; 1 John 4:16; Ephesians 2:4–5; Zephaniah 3:17; Jeremiah 31:3; 1 John 4:18; and Psalm 86:15. How does each verse speak to you in your season of *going through*?

____

____

____

____

____

____

____

____

____

____

____

As you choose to stop the insanity of striving and allow the Lord to fill the empty spots that only He can fill, there are things you can do daily to invite Him in to refresh your soul, fill the gaps, and wash away the need to do it for yourself. Here's a few that I do daily. It starts with first things first. First thing in the morning, I love Him with thanksgiving. This prepares my heart to focus on Him, rather than on my feelings or the circumstances of my day ahead. I open His Word and let His promises speak to my heart. I listen with stillness, wanting to receive whatever He wants to fill me with. I close in worship to express my love for Him and thank Him for loving me. I want to encourage you to take time each day to be with Him. As you do, how is He faithfully filling holes that were once desolate and dry?

____

____

____

____

____

____

____

There's a song I love, and I have a feeling the Samaritan woman would have loved it too. In fact, I can imagine her running around town and singing it for the rest of her days. It's one that I have made my mantra as well. It's called "Give Me Jesus." I love the version sung by Steffany Gretzinger and Jeremy Riddle on YouTube. Take time to listen. Allow Jesus to flood you with His life-giving water while you write about what He's doing so beautifully in you.

____

____

____

____

____

____

____

____

____

Going through causes chasms, too big for us to fill. The gaping holes of hurts, losses, and letdowns can only be filled by the One who restores, renews, and replenishes: Jesus. He is the One *for* the one. The One who goes out of His way to meet with the one who seems to be a no one to the world. He is the only One who satisfies. Go to Him. He is faithful to fill you up exceedingly and abundantly with life beyond your understanding, while recycling your pain into a very special purpose.

> *Thank the LORD for his faithful love and for the amazing things he*
>
> *does for people. He satisfies those who are thirsty. He fills those*
>
> *who are hungry with good things.*
>
> *(Psalm 107:8–9 ERV)*

CHAPTER 7

Prison

As time lagged on, week after week, my mom and dad fueled their faith on the Word of God, while I fired my thoughts, emotions, and life choices with fear, frustrations, and superficial, flimsy replacements. My anger raged toward the one who caused my world to unravel. Shackling my life to a chain of pain, turmoil, and unforgiveness that recoiled my being to an internal prison cell.

After six weeks of recovery, believe it or not, my dad was back to preaching at the pulpit of our church. The sanctuary was filled with people that morning prepared to hear my dad's heart and listen to the testimony relating to his supernatural survival and healing. Church attenders, people from the community, and those from our past sat knitted together in the pews, listening intently to every word he spoke. Even the primary person of interest in my father's case showed up, perched in the back row of the congregation. My dad stood before the parishioners and the crowd and publicly announced, with tears streaming down his face, his forgiveness toward the man who had shot him point-blank in the chest and desired him dead.

Every day turned into another dragging twenty-four hours of waiting for an update that would hopefully be a break in the case. However, after four long, grueling Michigan winter months, the police profile regarding the person of interest was made available to our family; it described the type of person who would do such a thing along with the motive behind their attack. As we read the details of the report, it homed in on the assailant's weapon of choice and why he chose it. A twelve-gauge shotgun was selected for its killing power, and the twelve-gauge slug was chosen for its destructive force.

That weapon of carnage and damaging strength did more than blow a hole through my dad's forty-five-year-old body; it invoked hatred in my soul, wanting justice for my unrest. The details of the assailant's personality on paper screamed narcissist and control freak. It revealed someone who could play it cool in public places and friendly to the world around him, but behind closed doors, he was a cold-blooded psychopath.

Fear intertwined with rage is a dangerous toxin, and it was brewing and boiling in the depths of my being. The profile of this criminal's characteristics just confirmed his inconsiderate, selfish, self-seeking, unpredictable, indifferent personality and his destructive ways. This character evaluation of the perpetrator answered none of my inquiries related to why this incident occurred in the first place, adding more heat to my toxic mess.

The offender had no consideration of who he was hurting; instead, he hoped to solve a significant personal problem he had, according to the psychological profile, by attempting to murder my father. The gunman believed my dad, a minister, knew too much about him. He thought it could be devastating to his reputation if whatever secrets he had would have become obtainable. So, taking my dad out was the only plausible solution he thought he had to ease his anxiety and concern. Fear seemed to be the intention behind the planned attack and the real root of the issue regarding this crime.

Fear has a repulsive, violating, and infectious way about it; it's a weakness that causes turmoil to one and spreads viciously to others through its careless and deceitful tactics. While the assailant's fear caused him to traumatize our family, it contagiously caused me to fall apart and shatter. My unpredictable choices and fickle behavior continued to wreck me, causing daily meltdowns and severe anxiety attacks. I was at my breaking point. And I knew I had to separate from the places, people, and things that were peppering my pain, everything I had run to, to fill my void.

I met with my parents, honestly and openly, and told them that I desperately needed help. I broke down before them, spilling my pain that filled my soul. They listened with compassion and a willingness to help. They contacted a Christian counselor for me to meet with weekly to start the process of *hopefully* healing my shredded and tattered heart.

My first visit with the therapist, I felt guarded and unsure of what to say or where to start. I listened as she talked about the steps we'd take *together*. Her kindness and quiet office, located forty-five minutes east of my hometown, allowed me the safety to be real. It was far enough away from my daily living, giving me a boundary and a break from the place my haunted memories stirred about and the sights where my infected wounds continuously ripped opened.

The therapist spoke first, to start the session, saying, "Let's get started," and I broke apart like a clay pot shattered into a thousand pieces on the floor. Tears poured out from my eyes like rain during hurricane season in the tropics. I talked and ranted and went on and on about things I'm not sure made *any* sense. Her gentle eyes and simple nods revealed her compassion and sympathy for my aching soul. Talking to an outsider was exactly what I needed, someone who could see the big picture without any personal involvement or connection to the pain I had been living through. As we closed our first session, she prayed for me, and that simple prayer meant *everything*.

As I left her office that day, I learned something I will never forget: the value and importance of a listening ear. An open ear that listens without judgment and meets a person in *their* pain is quite rare and precious. However, I had no clue what I'd shared with her or even if it made any sense at all. I knew at least one thing: I left her office a little bit lighter than when I arrived. I had dropped some of my burdens off at her door, and that seemed to alleviate some of my heavy load.

I continued to meet with the therapist weekly, until I felt some relief from the PTSD I had endured. I made some changes to my life to help bring balance to my being and encourage my health—mentally, emotionally, and physically. And although I walked away from some of my bad habits while upheaving my burdens on a counselor, I was still lacking the most pivotal thing to freeing my enslaved soul.

Time waits for no one, they say, and as time marched on, the dreaded months of my nightmare turned into years with no resolution. My dad's shooting became an unsolved mystery over time. A news story with no answers, no explanation, and no justice. A senseless crime that did more damage than people could really see or understand. Time, of course, brought some healing, but I still carried a prison of fear, anger, and hatred buried deep inside of me.

I had learned to keep my emotions under wraps by doing life superficially like other twenty-something-year-olds. I worked, attended college, hung out with friends, and partied, a lot. This kept things shallow and not too serious. I knew my own boundaries after my breakdowns, so living superficially like other young adults made me feel more normal, as if I had never gone through what I had gone through.

I found out rather quickly, this kind of shallow living has consequences. Running around with no direction or purpose didn't dissipate the prison cell; instead, it welcomed more chains and pain. And that's exactly what I did and exactly what I found. I greeted and invited, up close and personal, more bondage and oppression within my prison cell, which nobody saw.

I got involved with someone who also had chains, an insecure man with a prison cell surrounding his heart as large as mine, if not larger. I was looking for love in all the wrong places. His narcissism controlled our relationship, along with every little thing I said and did. My confinement was no longer hidden in the depths of my heart; it now became the reality of my entire being, inside and out.

His control influenced everything—where I went, where I worked, whom I called a friend (or not), and whom I was allowed to be close to.

This relationship shook off any strength I thought I had. It left me feeling crazy and constantly questioning my fault in our fights. It kept me submissive and small, holding my breath for the next trial I would be put on before his judgmental eyes and verbally abusive tongue. His custody kept me in line until one night, he beat me up. His abusive words were one thing, but his fierce fist, infused with alcohol, was another.

Friends were in the other room when the brawl began, so they could hear his shouts and the loud sound of someone hitting a wall. I pried open the bathroom door and ran for my life. A friend followed me and drove me to the hospital to be examined and then to the police department to file a domestic violence report.

I moved back home with my parents that very night. In my naïveté, I held on to a sliver of hope for healing this unstable relationship with this broken man. His charm and apologies persuaded me he was changing. As we sought counseling and help, he committed himself to stop drinking, while I had the surprise shock of finding out I was pregnant.

My pregnancy proved everything. During my first six months of morning sickness, visits to the hospital for dehydration while getting physically bigger each month, swollen feet, and lack of sleep, my supposedly committed partner was off doing his thing, living it up like a bachelor—doing just the opposite of his promised pledge.

It was the loneliest time of my life, I must admit, but also the quiet and contemplative season I desperately needed for clarity and discernment. It was a time where the fog was finally lifting and I was beginning to see things as they were, for the first time. No more relying on alcohol to wash away my pain, no more fake friendships to fill my time, and no more superficial lifestyle choices with no purpose or intention. I found myself alone *a lot*, rehashing my old life in comparison to the fresh adventure and mystery of what was to come. I had a new role now. I was going to be a mom, and being a mom meant I had to think about someone else for a change. It was no longer just about me.

I spent a lot of sleepless nights pondering the previous five years: the choices I'd made, the hardships I'd endured, and the pointless places where I'd sought fulfillment. My mind was sober, and my heart was ready to surrender everything, even the prison I personally decorated with my own pain. I was ready to be done. I wanted to be set free. I was desperate to be alive again. I desired to live with hope. I yearned for joy. And I longed for real love that wouldn't run around on me like the ones I had experienced before.

As I lay in bed one night, a pillow between my knees to keep my pregnant belly from throwing me off the bed, I prayed a simple yet hesitant prayer to Jesus. He was someone I knew personally as a child, but I walked away from Him as a teenager because of silly distractions, ugly offenses, and enticing yet unfulfilling worldly junk. I began to understand in that moment, as I lay there, that I had begun building the prison deep inside me the moment I'd walked away from Jesus, years earlier. I pointed fingers and played the blame game for my own self-defense. But in reality, as I spent time finding fault and accusing people who had hurt me and the places that had caused me pain, I missed the fact that those prison bars were personally constructed by me, myself, and I.

That night it all made sense, in the quiet and stillness. My words in prayer came out sincerely as the truth gently rose up in me. My prayer wasn't hesitant because I didn't trust Him—no, it was actually just the opposite. My prayer was cautious because I wasn't sure *He* could trust *me*. My past had a track record of pain, instability, selfishness, and self-seeking desires that allowed my hurts to dictate my decisions. A pursuit of drowning out my problems in my own way, bouncing around, without loyalty to anything or anyone. I would take and grab, stingy and tightfisted, what I needed and wanted to bring me what I desperately

desired: wholeness. However, I seemed to neglect the only One who could

actually bring it.

Jesus, if I'm going to do this life with You, I want the real deal, okay? I

wept while I prayed. I didn't want a relationship out of duty or a legalistic

affiliation with Him. I wanted a real, sincere, down-to-earth, and personal

closeness with Jesus, the One I had loved with all my heart as child. And the One

I knew loved me too. *I give my life to You, I want to start over, let's do this

thing—together!* I felt His whisper in my heart, as real as the day is long: *I've

been waiting for you! Let's do this—together!*

In that moment, I felt a freedom unlike anything I had ever felt before. I

released to Him my deep, dark secrets of pain that had been confining me and

keeping me from feeling fully alive. I sensed Him taking my hand as I offered it

to Him, and tears swelled my eyes. He began to walk me through the healing and

the breakthrough I was truly ready to receive. He exposed what doing this

together really meant: He would be my everything while I simply clung to Him

(John 15).

He highlighted to me the first bricks that I had used to begin building my

own prison cell years before this mess got out of control. Offense and unforgiveness, two tools the devil uses to suck faith, joy, hope, love, and life out of a human being faster than a mosquito's bite. Jesus began showing me how to forgive and the healing power of letting go.

As I dug into God's Word to follow Jesus's steps as well as the example He set of stopping to meet needs, forgiveness was illuminated on every single page. I started to understand: the only way I am able to forgive others is by recognizing and acknowledging *His* choice to forgive me. Something He did lovingly and sacrificially on the cross, without delay or regret, laying down His life for mine, already knowing ahead of time all about my pushback and prideful, self-seeking, stingy ways and desires. He did this with great love for you and me.

I was quickly discovering that God's way of doing things was completely opposite of what my flesh desired and my feelings sought. I found out firsthand that forgiveness is first a choice before it is a feeling. Letting go was something my flesh fought and battled. However, as I *chose* to forgive and let go, the feelings followed, bringing liberty and melting chains and bars I once kept poised with anger and pride. I began to see that doing life with Him meant freedom and wholeness in ways I could never discover anywhere else.

This journey with Him liberated me to let go of the guilt and shame I directed toward myself as well as toward the people I was offended by when I chose to walk away from Jesus as a teenager. This also meant that I could release my anger toward the perpetrator who shot my dad, even without justice being served. I no longer had to live with the pain and rage fueled by the fear that had consumed his soul and later dangerously infected my own. I could now relinquish my hurts from the abuse and betrayal of the man I had once committed myself to, releasing him from my bitter clutch regardless of his apology or repentance. I let go, freeing him to go the direction he chose while I sought God's heart and will for my life, for I was determined to move on with God's peace.

I was beginning to find freedom in the midst of my circumstance, and it was invigorating to my entire being. My prison was finally dissolving. It disintegrated into *nothing*. My chains fell off and shattered. My past of haunted hurts and memories began to be erased; the yuck I held on to started to evaporate. My life was now brand-new, and each day now had hope infused with joy, peace, and purpose. God's real love held on to me firmly, leading my every step while He saw the gold in me that I couldn't see for myself.

My faith steps were tiny as I pursued God's heart; however, He didn't seem to be too concerned with how big or small my treads were. He was just there, in every tiptoe, encouraging me along the way, holding my hand through the small shuffles that slowly turned into exciting strides with Him leading the way. And over time my faith grew in leaps and bounds as I chose to trust Him with details I never had before. He began to write my new story, one that He had written for me, inscribing it on my heart and sealing it in my spirit. I was seeing clearly for the first time: He was with me always, even in the midst of my *going through*.

No more prison walls built by my pain or empty gaps hollowed out by my hurts or my shallow, complacent choices. I had finally surrendered to the One who replaced all that. The One who generously provided the freedom even when I didn't feel like I deserved it. He was redesigning and restructuring my new foundation in Him with His plentiful and extravagant love.

My *going through* season taught me that fear is infectious and spreadable, but I also discovered God's love is more contagious. As 1 John 4:16–17 (ERV) says, "So we know the love that God has for us, and we trust that love. God is love. Everyone who lives in love lives in God, and God lives in them. If God's love is made perfect in us, we can be without fear on the day when God judges the world. We will be without fear, because in this world we are like Jesus."

While you continue through this chapter, it's okay to ponder your own soul condition. Are your prison bars and bricks revealing themselves? What has caused you to construct them? How do you keep them as strong as iron, fierce and foundational? When did they start going up? Who or what have you blamed them on? How is your prison cell spilling over into your daily life and into the life God is calling you to?

As you ponder these things on paper, let's take a look at someone who's encouraged me along the way. A man in the Bible whose internal prison wreaked havoc on many but who miraculously broke open from the confinement of pain and pride, freeing himself to live out God's purpose and to see the gold God saw in him. God has a way of seeing our destiny even when we can't. He calls us to it by seeing the treasure we never could. And this man's life speaks profoundly of this truth. Join me as we take a look at Saul (aka Paul) in the New Testament.

Acts 8 gives us an introduction to his life. You can join me there so you can see all the fascinating details. His existence was so entrenched in a prison of his own way of doing and thinking, he deceived himself into believing he was undertaking God's will. He was stirred up by his own cause, one that God never called him to. Saul found himself the ringleader of the cabal that imprisoned others as well as himself. His murderous threats and eager spirit to lock up and kill those who threatened his way of living seemed to be embedded with fear.

But then one day everything changed. Saul met Jesus with one simple conversation. Acts 9 highlights the details gloriously. The light that had been void in his life now illuminated his trembling body as the voice of Jesus beckoned him and questioned his decisions. This is a beautiful reminder to us. Jesus has such a wonderful and intentional way of meeting us personally right where we are. Jesus met me—lonely, hopeless, angry, broken, and pregnant, lying in a bed—and He met Saul—hateful, vindictive, and on a determined and murderous mission to imprison and kill.

Well, Saul's life got turned upside down and inside out—in a really good way, of course. One heart-to-heart with Jesus started a domino effect. As you finish Acts 9 and continue through this book, you can see how Saul's life transformed completely: he went from murderer to missionary in a matter of days. As we see throughout the New Testament, his adventures unfolded through a series of beatings, rejections, trials, a shipwreck, and even imprisonment. And interestingly enough, his *going through* had everything to do with his faith in Jesus Christ. Nevertheless, his perspective about *going through* brought depth and insight that confronted my faith, taking it to deeper levels and inflicting a new way of understanding as I went through my various *going through* seasons.

In fact, if we shadow Saul (Paul) through Philippians 1:12–18, what caused his confinement? ____

____

What were his chains allowing him to do? _______________________________

____

____

____

How does Paul's outlook impact you? ___________________________________

____

____

____

Head on over to 2 Corinthians 12:7–10. What was Paul's new understanding of

his weakness? ____

____

____

What caused him to be glad? ____

____

____

____

Who was really his strength? _______________________________

And how does that go completely against our fleshly feelings? _______________

____

____

____

Lastly, let's look at Philippians 4:10–13. What had Paul learned about

contentment? _______________________________________

____

____

____

Who really was his satisfaction and wholeness? _______________________

How does this shake your attitude and stance, your personal insight and

understanding? _______________________________________

____

____

____

I hope you're seeing it all clearly: the tremendous power of one dialogue

with Jesus has lasting repercussions. It only takes one chat with Jesus to change

everything. And that one discussion starts a chain reaction of unlocking bars that imprison souls. It's one heart-to-heart that brings wholeness and freedom where no one or nothing else could. My life is living proof of this. So is Paul's.

What about you? Are you ready to be set free? Are you wanting to let go? Are you desperate to speak with the One who holds the keys that can liberate you from your fears, your pride, and your pain? Are you tired of holding on to offenses and unforgiveness? Are you ready for the bricks to be brought down?

If so, take this very moment to speak directly to the One who can do all this—Jesus. Let your heart break open with repentance. Allow the pain to flow out and the chains to fall off. Ask Him in. Welcome His presence. Give Him all of you. Ask Him for all of Him. Allow this conversation to be real and raw, authentic and genuine. Talk to Him openly while you listen with earnest and eager attention. This one conversation with Him will change everything.

Reflection Questions:

What's been constructing the prison cell in your soul—fear, hatred, anger, hurt, rejection? How long have the walls been up? How have you been maintaining the bars that keep you locked in and knocked down? Feel free to be honest as you let it all out on the lines below.

____

____

____

____

____

____

____

____

____

____

How has your prison cell kept you confined? How has it dictated your decisions and life choices? How has it distracted you from the One who can free you from the chains?

Are you ready and willing to have that one conversation with Jesus, the one that changes everything? The one where you welcome Him to hold your hand and lead, while leaving your mess at His feet? If so, let Him know as you share your heart with Him. If you're unsure of what to say, pray the simple prayer I did, with a cry of desperation and your need for Him: "I give my life to You, I want to start over, let's do this thing—together!" As you surrender, what is He telling you in the stillness of your time together?

____

____

____

____

____

____

____

____

____

Take some time to study who Paul was before he met Jesus in Acts 7 through Acts 8:1–3, then jump over to Acts 16:16–40 to one scenario that reveals who he became after he met Jesus. What prison was Paul in before he met Jesus? What words would you use to describe his heart before his conversion? As you study the details of Acts 16, how was Paul completely different? He was a murderer turned missionary, Jesus-lover, and worshipper; his life and words eventually declared his heart after Jesus! How does Paul's freedom encourage and inspire you in your *going through* journey?

____

____

____

____

____

____

____

____

Just as Jesus transformed Paul, He can transform you. He will teach you how to love and live again, how to hope and forgive, how to find freedom in letting go, and how to receive all that He has for you. Write down the areas where you need His help the most.

Take some time to meditate on who He really is to you as you start this fresh journey with Him. Fill the lines with your gratitude. Be encouraged by the following worship tunes as you contemplate His goodness in your journey together: "Let it Happen" by United Pursuit, "Better Than" by Bethel Music and Jonathan David and Melissa Helser, "Who You Say I Am" by Hillsong Worship, "I Thank God" by Maverick City Music, "Reckless Love" by Cory Asbury, "Defender" by Jesus Culture, "Oceans" by Coffey Anderson, "No Longer Slaves" by Bethel Music, "Mercy" by Elevation Worship and Maverick City Music, "Breakthrough" by Chris McClarney, "Closer" by Bethel Music and Steffany Gretzinger, and "I Want Jesus" by Jesus Image and John Wilds.

____

____

____

____

____

____

____

Going through entices self-defense in us, building barricades and bars to protect our wounded souls. Prison cells erected create more chains while bricks of offense and unforgiveness keep us from our destiny. There is only One who can truly heal and bring wholeness. There is only One who can melt away our iron-clad construction of fear and agony while helping us to free the ones we blame. Jesus. Only Him. And just one conversation with Him changes everything.

> *The Spirit of the Sovereign LORD is upon me, for the LORD has anointed me to bring good news to the poor. He has sent me to comfort the brokenhearted and to proclaim that captives will be released and prisoners will be freed.*
>
> *(Isaiah 61:1 NLT)*

CHAPTER 8

Eyes Wide Open

"Where was God?" This has been a weighty and reflective question my family and I have been asked over the last twenty-six years in regard to my dad's shooting on October 27, 1996. In my *going through*, I couldn't quite answer this question because it was a question that required me to look beyond my perspective. It wasn't possible for me to answer for God's whereabouts in this when I could only see through my human lens. To answer this question required more than what I had at the time; it required faith.

You may be wondering the same thing. Where is God in your *going through*? Why can't you see Him? Why don't you feel Him? Your cries may have turned to shouts of, "Where are You, God?" as you battle through this difficult season in your life. Well, as you follow me through this closing chapter, I pray you find your answer, the way that I have found mine with eyes wide open.

Eyes wide open? You may be wondering, *What in the world does that mean?* Well, here's the best way I know how to describe it: It's a faith-filled perspective that only God can give. It's a supernatural view that He generously offers us, even in our *going through.* It's insight that our human minds and flesh can't quite comprehend or understand, especially in our dark and difficult seasons. However, God is more ready and willing to pour out His divine presence, awareness, and wisdom even in our *going through* seasons especially when we ask Him sincerely. It's taken faith for me to step out, to surrender my sight fully, so that I can see that God is a gracious and compassionate God who loves to provide, pursue, and fulfill; He loves to lavish us with His extravagant understanding and profound love, and all we need to do is seek and ask (Matthew 6:33; Matthew 7:7; James 1:5).

Hindsight is always twenty-twenty, or so they say. I've come to appreciate this saying more fully in my faith journey. And although my *going through* has confronted the depths of my being, my perspective, my faith, and even my will to survive at times, I have now discovered God's whereabouts in every single detail, and it has required a full yielding from me.

"Lord, please open my eyes! Give me eyes wide open! Let me see Your perspective in my *going through*." This has been my heart's prayer and cry because I know my lens is small and sorrowful, but His view is filled with purpose and promise. He brings beauty from ashes and joy instead of tears of grief (Isaiah 61:3). I have found I am desperate for this promise. I am starving for

His view and His vision. Are you too? As you draw close to Him and ask for His eyes, His faithfulness will astound you, you'll see.

God's Word is clear and concise. It reveals the beauty of asking God for His view and reveals His faithful provision—seeing through His sovereign lens—a supernatural perspective that changes everything about our tough times. I pray the truth of His Word encourages, amazes, and baffles you as we dig deeper and look more specifically at a compelling illustration of God's perspective found in 2 Kings 6:8–17.

I'll help set the stage for this story as best as I can. The enemies of Israel were constantly in a race to trap the Israelites and immobilize them. This was ongoing throughout the Old Testament. The Israelites always had some group of people fighting against them. However, in this specific chapter, Elisha, a man of God, seemed to have the intel, insight, and understanding to know the enemies' secret plans to their every move.

If you haven't heard of Elisha yet, his story is a must-read! The details of his narrative begin in 1 Kings 19. I want to encourage you to dive in, headfirst, and read about his wild and amazing ventures with God. The power of Jesus oozes from his life and fires up my faith to deeper levels! I know it will for you as well! Okay, let's jump back to 2 Kings 6!

In order to provide safety to the Israeli troops, Elisha supernaturally warned the king of Israel time and time again of their enemies' tactics. It was astounding wisdom and insight that God gave Elisha to help God's chosen people remain safe from those who wanted to defeat them. Elisha was given God's glorious perspective—eyes wide open—to help God's people in their *going through.*

The Aramean king started to get pretty upset over this, and rightfully so! Every plan, scheme, and trick to attack the Israelites would be ruined in an instant. The Aramean king began to confront his own men, accusing them of being traitors, because he couldn't quite figure out how the Israeli troops always knew their whereabouts.

In 2 Kings 6:12, we see that one of the king's officers finally revealed what was really going on, as he shares with the king his fascinating finds in regard to this prophet, Elisha, from Israel. There was no spy or traitor in the Aramean camp, just a prophet in Israel who tells the Israeli king everything—"even what you say in your bedroom" (2 Kings 6:12 GW). This outraged the Aramean king! So, instead of setting up camp to prepare for battle against Israel again, the king of Aram decides to trick this prophet by sending his army straight to Dothan to seize Elisha (dun, dun, dun!)

As Elisha slept soundly that night, the great and mighty Aramean army showed up and surrounded Dothan with war horses and intimidating chariots, ready to take Elisha out. As Elisha's servant awakened early the next morning and glanced outside, he saw the mammoth Aramean troops, horses, and chariots surrounding them. I can picture the servant's freaked-out expression, his eyes getting really big, his jaw dropping to the ground, and his heart racing with anxiety as the vast army overwhelmed his view.

I'm sure it didn't take the servant too long to get Elisha's attention concerning this problem. Second Kings 6:15 (MSG) reveals his desperate plea: "The young man exclaimed, "Oh, master! What shall we do?" Can you imagine the servant's fear and concern? I have a feeling his mind began to scatter about with his own escape plan. *Hmm . . . should we sneak out the back window, hide under a table, or pretend we're not here?* I'm sure his fear paralyzed his faith and his logic. The servant could only see what was before him, his own reality—the Aramean army versus him and Elisha—and there was no hope to be found.

But just then, Elisha answers back, "Don't be afraid. We have more forces on our side than they have on theirs" (2 Kings 6:16 GW). I imagine the servant's head tilted with intrigued confusion as Elisha's statement spoken with complete confidence. Then Elisha did the simple thing we all seem to forget to do in our *going through*. It's something we tend to blow off and not make our first priority . . . Elisha prayed. His prayer was an earnest one-liner, a pivotal request that spoke volumes to the kingdom of heaven; it declared a 9-1-1 desperation for a God who was big enough to answer the call. "LORD, please open his eyes so that he may see" (2 Kings 6:17 GW). And just like that, a simple, sincere prayer was answered by God Almighty. "The LORD opened the servant's eyes and let him see. The mountain around Elisha was full of fiery horses and chariots" (2 Kings 6:17 GW).

The Lord gave the servant eyes wide open. A perspective of where God really was—surrounding them with forces much greater and much more visible than the servant could see from his human lens. Eyes to see beyond his circumstance. Eyes to see God's whereabouts in the trouble. It's interesting to note also that Elisha didn't pray for God to change the situation; he only prayed that his servant could see the reality of the situation. Yes, trouble surrounded them. Yes, fear and doubt confronted them, and yes, the *going through* was about to seize them and take them out. However, that was not the full reality of their situation or the ending to their story. Once Elisha sincerely asked for the servant's eyes to be opened, the Lord responded and allowed the servant to truly see God's glorious view.

God's army was there, with them, in the midst of it all. God's angelic military outnumbered and overpowered the enemy army that tried to come against them. Elisha didn't have to convince the servant of this reality with his words either; instead, Elisha prayed and asked God to allow the servant to see for himself God's whereabouts. And guess what? This same exact opportunity applies to us as well. All we have to do is ask.

Eyes wide open. This is my prayer for you. As you walk through this challenging season you face, may the Lord open your eyes to the reality of your situation. May you see His whereabouts in your *going through.* May you understand He is for you; He is the One who has your back, He is your strength, He is your salvation, He is your peace, and He is your hope.

My hope is that you can see as clearly as Elisha's servant that day along with Balaam in Numbers 24. May the Spirit of God come upon you so that you can distinctly see His truth. God Almighty, the five-star general of the angel armies of heaven, surrounds you right where you are, in your *going through* (Psalm 27). May you see Him fully and encounter His presence, insight, love, and understanding abundantly and supernaturally as you pursue His perspective in your *going through.*

Well, the mysterious answers you may have hoped to receive as I close out my story may not be what you were expecting. After twenty-six years, justice, in an earthly sense, was never served. The person who shot my dad was never found or arrested. There was no hearing or trial or closure through the justice system that I can tell you about. There were no finite answers or profound discoveries, no resolution or conclusion. In fact, this crime remains an unsolved mystery to this day, according to the justice system.

While my eyes used to be fixed on my need to receive this closure and for justice to be served, God was bringing me something far greater—*His* freedom, *His* righteousness, *His* healing, *His* forgiveness, and *His* understanding, something no one or nothing else in this world could ever bring. God was actually moving, working, and performing implausible miracles all around me and even inside me. And although I couldn't see Him very clearly at times in the midst of my *going through*, because my eyes were fixed elsewhere, eventually I found His presence as I sought His view.

I have received *His* beauty for my ashes. I have found *His* grace undeservedly. I now have a renewed heart and mind in Christ, a fresh perspective. And I can't escape the simple and seemingly small intricate details that God has pieced together, all the numerous miracles that have taken place amid my *going through*. These weren't just coincidences or fortuity; these supernatural occurrences have revealed God's hand of hope in a timely manner and in certain specifics that only a supernatural God could orchestrate.

"Where was God?" I now know the answer. He was right there with me, in my every step, every breath, every second, and in my every detail, faithfully holding my hand, amid my *going through*. This is *how* God turns tragedy into triumph. As we *go through* difficulties and challenges, He's right there holding us, in love, as we choose to cling to Him, we discover His glorious presence even in our pain and His presence changes *everything*. As I share the following miracles with you, I pray that you can see God's whereabouts in your *going through*, as you see God's location in mine with eyes wide open.

Seventeen years before my dad's shooting, my dad's lungs were burnt. He had only 39 percent of his breathing due to a factory job he had before becoming a minister. As a result, many of my childhood memories include hearing my dad violently coughing from his bathroom every single morning. His coughing spells would leave him spewing up blood each day to relieve the inflammation in his chest.

In January of 1996, ten months before my dad's shooting, he and my mom attended a pastors' conference in Michigan. One of the services held a time of forgiveness and healing for the ministers who gathered. My dad decided to go up for prayer for his lungs, something he felt he had done a million times before when an opportunity to be prayed for was offered. After this prayer, my dad went back to his seat, not feeling any different but thanking the Lord for His continual faithfulness.

The weekend after the conference, my parents joined friends from church for a January sleigh ride in the local park. The Michigan weather was frigid, with the outdoor temperature at approximately twenty degrees. My mom began to notice something peculiar in my dad's breathing as they walked down the road in the cold, crisp air toward the sleigh ride. Then it hit her, and joy burst from her heart as she pronounced, "Honey, your lungs are healed!"

Cold weather always caused my dad to breathe harder and heavier, but my mom, as a nurse, could see and hear that his breathing was absolutely normal in the twenty-degree weather! My dad literally began to leap and jump around on the frozen path that day, something he hadn't been able to do for seventeen years! He realized in that moment: his lungs were completely healed! My parents praised the Lord and shared the good news with everyone they saw. If my dad's lungs had not been healed then, his survival from the shooting ten months later would have been slim to none. We're praising the Lord for this God-timely miracle!

And there's more!

After the shooting, the doctor wanted my dad's lungs tested, since the shooting caused one of his lungs to collapse, while the other lung filled with blood. The doctors wanted to be sure his lungs were functioning properly after all the trauma to his chest cavity. The tests came back with an amazing result! My dad, forty-five years old, received a score of 139 percent! This reflected the lung health and the lung capacity of a thirty-year-old! God *literally* gave my dad his breathing back, even above and beyond where they had been before! We were blown away by God's abundance and goodness!

As the Lord continued to open my eyes, I was seeing more and more of His extravagant presence in my *going through*. Our family's conversations reminded us that before the shooting, on Sunday mornings around five a,m. my dad was most often found in his church office, praying and seeking the Lord before the morning service. However, because of my sister's wedding the night before, my dad had scheduled a guest speaker for Sunday's service. During the investigation that morning, the church doors were found ajar and his office light left on with the door wide open. The investigators believe the gunman, with his twelve-gauge shotgun, expected to meet my dad that morning in his church office, alone and without anyone able to call for help after a confrontational and murderous shot. Because the gunman didn't find my dad in his office, they believe the gunman went to our home to complete his mission.

The fact that my sister and I were at home that Sunday morning when this event occurred was likely quite surprising to the gunman. As teenagers, we were at friends' houses quite a bit for sleepovers and such. We were always on the go! If my sister and I had not been home that morning, who knows what the outcome could have been? Could my mom have handled the stress and the pressure of that morning alone? Would she have been able to get the help my dad needed? Only God knows.

The Holy Spirit's providence in that morning was so surreal. He filled my mom, sister, and me with His grace, His strength, and His empowerment to do what it took to retrieve help for my dad that morning. It was all the Holy Spirit at work in us and through us. There was no way I could have been bold enough, brave enough, wise enough, or strong enough, in my own power, to leave our house for help that morning. My little sister, Leah, could not have held the towels over my dad's dying body without God's presence supporting her. The Holy Spirit gave her the grace and wisdom to speak words of life over him and gave my dad hope to receive them in the midst of death devouring him. My mom was able to make decisions clearly and consciously that morning because of God's discernment, wisdom, and clarity at work in her. Only God's Spirit, His power and presence, accomplished the things we needed to do that frightful and unforgettable morning.

I have also been reminded that my dad had always been a light sleeper. Any noise he heard in the night, he would typically wake up and walk around the house to check on everything. My family and I have discussed what that could have looked like if he had gotten up that morning, if he had heard the perpetrator enter our home. The various scenarios have floored our thinking. Any standing position could have more likely brought death instantaneously if my dad had met the gunman roaming around the house.

We truly believe my dad's body positioning in his bed that morning was God ordained and planned. The way my dad's body was situated, as he stretched his hand out to halter the slug, was divinely influenced. If my dad had been lying flat down, he would have more likely died immediately. The impact of the slug through his body along with the compression of the bed below him could have trapped the slug in his chest, causing more damage and possibly imminent death. In my dad's sleepiness, the Lord aligned his body in such a way that the slug could not terminate any vital organs in his chest. His positioning allowed the slug to exit freely out of his body. Both doctors and police have presumed this as well.

My dad's positioning that morning may have also saved *my* life. I slept in the bedroom next to my parents. My bed was parallel to the wall where my parents' heads were. Their bed was perpendicular to mine; the wall divided our rooms. If my dad had sat straight up, as the gunman pulled the trigger, the slug that entered his chest could have gone through the wall next to me. However, because of my dad's slight turn toward the left, the slug went through the right side of his body and exited out the front wall of our home, adjacent to the wall that connected our rooms. The slug was found buried in our front yard during the investigation the week of the shooting. We continue to be amazed by God's hand in the seemingly smallest and greatest of details.

The timing of the shooting in relation to the timing of my dad receiving medical help is quite interesting as well. Since our phone lines were cut by the intruder, it seemed to have taken a while for us to figure out a way to call for help in our traumatized state. The police were the first to arrive on the scene. The ambulance was not willing to come as quickly, because the 9-1-1 call revealed it was a shooting. Paramedics would not show up unless they had the clear from the police that the surroundings were safe.

The policeman who arrived on the scene first saw the criticality of my dad's condition. My dad's pain, thrashing, the death rattle in his chest along with his blood loss provoked the policeman to yell at the paramedics to get to the scene immediately. My dad was shot at approximately five that morning; however, the ambulance did not take him to the hospital until *after* the sun came up, which was at 7:03 a.m. in Milford, Michigan, that day. Plus, when the ambulance finally did arrive, the hospital was about nine to ten miles from our home, adding an extra seventeen to twenty minutes for my dad to receive the full medical attention he needed at the hospital. During the two hours of suffering without full medical attention, my dad never lost consciousness even though he lost seven pints of blood. God sustained my dad's life that morning.

When my dad arrived at the hospital, there was one surgeon on staff who was about to complete his shift and leave for home. He was also considered to be the best surgeon in the hospital. As the paramedics urgently rolled my dad through the emergency hallway, the medical staff transferred him immediately into the surgical room, where they prepped my dad for surgery.

My dad remembers the chatter among the medical staff as they wondered who and why someone would shoot a man in his home, on a dark, eerie morning, in a sleepy and boring town like Milford. Questions about my dad's reputation arose, while the medical staff rambled on and on about the possible reasons something like this would happen. As my dad's consciousness went fuzzy due to the anesthesia administered into his body for surgery, his heart was grieved by

their disheartening jabbering, but there was something more going on behind the

scenes that my parents discovered later about that morning in the surgical room.

When my parents arrived at my dad's first appointment with the surgeon

after he was eventually released from the hospital, a nurse called my parents into

the exam room. She shut the door behind them, sat down, and started to cry. She

began explaining that she was one of the nurses who attended my dad's surgery

the morning of the shooting. With tears streaming down her face, she described

the profound details of what had occurred that morning. As the surgeon walked

into the operating room, he looked around with a quiet and serene confidence; he

then asked the medical staff a surprising and strange question, followed by a

profound statement. "Can you feel that? This is a man of God, and everything is

going to be all right."

The tangible presence of God filled the room so intensely that morning

that no one could deny it. It was strong, thick, peaceful, and powerful. The nurse

cried as she shared the sweet details of God's presence and weighty peace that

filled the environment as my dad's life hung in the balance. Amid the gossip and

accusations pointed at my dad that morning in the surgical room, the Holy Spirit suppressed the lies and the chatter, and instead brought His overwhelming peace and insurmountable power to the room and stunned the entire medical staff.

My dad's recovery in itself was astounding! Surviving a blast from a shotgun that close and missing vital organs that could have brought death instantaneously all seemed incredibly insane and far-fetched! But it was as if God Himself supernaturally maneuvered that slug through my dad's body.

My dad endured eight hours of surgical repair and beat the odds of death, with the high risk of peritonitis. He was discharged from the hospital in just ten days. Even as my dad was healing, he felt the Holy Spirit reveal to him the importance of drinking lots of water. As he did, the medical staff was astonished by his unbelievable quick recovery. Only God could do that! In fact, my dad's only complaint from the shooting had nothing to do with the shooting itself; instead, it was the hemorrhoids (go figure!) he endured from sitting so much during his healing.

My mom also experienced a providential healing. My mom lived for a long time with the fear of thinking the intruder was following her each time she left our home. Her mind raced with anxiety thinking that the gunman would come back to finish the job, to take my dad and her out with one last blow.

One evening, while my mom drove home, the evening sky set in. She found herself on a dirt road overcome with worry as she approached a four-way stop. A car pulled up behind her with its headlights shining through her back window, illuminating off her side and rearview mirrors. She froze in fear at the stop sign, thinking this was it—the intruder had followed her to this stop sign so he could complete the job. But just then, my mom felt a dome of light surround her, a supernatural light encompassing her like a cocoon. The peace of God filled her up from head to toe. She felt the whisper of the Lord, so sweet, yet affirmative and direct, say to her, *No one can hurt you. They would have to go through Me first!* In that moment my mom knew she no longer had to live with that paralyzing fear. She knew instantaneously that God was her defense, her shield, and her strength (Psalm 28:7).

The Lord gave my mom a supernatural faith, healing her from her fear, insecurity, and worry in regard to the intrusion. God encouraged her and empowered her with His profound peace that transcended all of her own understanding (Philippians 4:7). She was filled with God's boldness, truth, authority, and rest. A peace that only Jesus can bring.

God was continually working in the midst of unanswered questions, and His peace was becoming more and more real as I sought Him. He was revealing so beautifully *His* whereabouts in *my* struggle. His presence was becoming more evident as I watched Him move in our story and encourage others in theirs.

As my dad recovered, he was asked to share his story of the shooting at a family friend's small church plant. After the church service, while the staff, leaders, and volunteers were cleaning up and reloading the truck, my dad asked the pastor and his wife if there was anything that he could pray for them about. The pastor was about to sputter out his prayer needs, such as church growth, more money, and all the desperate requests that come with having a small church plant; however, instead, his wife, in tenacious faith, blurted out, "Our son has autism, and we want to see him healed!" This statement surprised her, even as it came out, because they both, as a couple, had quit praying for their son's healing. They had become very weary and discouraged in doing so. So my dad, in agreement with this pastor and his wife, laid hands on their four-and-a-half-year-old son with autism, on the loading dock of the school that day. My dad prayed a simple prayer of healing over the young boy. As he prayed, he shared with them, "God told me He's going to heal your son for His glory. You've seen Him as a loving God, but He's going to show you, He's a powerful God." And immediately after the prayer, the son looked up at his parents and said, "Hi, Dad!" with full eye contact and complete clarity.

The parents declared that their son came alive over the next few weeks! His healing was confirmed as he began interacting with others, communicating clearly, using eye contact, and responding in ways the little boy never had before. Today, this young man, who once had autism, is completely healed. He is a minister, happily married and expecting his first child. This young man experienced complete healing from autism for one reason and one reason alone—God's glory!

I knew fear was contagious, but God was revealing to me, up close and personal, that His love, goodness, and presence are even more contagious. The Lord continued to use my dad's testimony of God's supernatural saving grace, healing power, and forgiveness to encourage and minister to others, while bringing complete glory to Himself! The Lord's mighty hand was alive and real, working in ways *my* physical eyes could not comprehend. It was changing the way I saw everything!

Years later my dad was invited to meet with a pastor in Michigan who was *going through* a traumatic and challenging situation himself. The pastor had been stabbed numerous times by an intruder who had broken into his home. The minister woke up to confront the thief and scare him off but was instead brutally attacked at knifepoint.

As my dad sat with the hurting minister in the hospital, they talked for hours. It's a lonely place when you face a situation where your life is threatened by another, and although Jesus completely understands, it's nice to have Jesus friends who completely understand the trauma and sorrow too. The two of them spent time processing the pain together and looking for Jesus in the details.

My dad shared with him his own journey of forgiveness and the healing power of the Word of God, which had brought our family through *our* ordeal. My dad described it as a key ingredient to be able to move forward and experience all that God was up to. Since then, this pastor has been healed by God—physically, emotionally, mentally, and spiritually—God is now using him to minister to others about the power of forgiveness.

To this day my mom and dad continue to share the wild and wondrous miracles surrounding God's goodness in the midst of life's circumstances. The testimonies of this *going through*, which tried to kill, steal, and destroy my dad's life, my mom's faith, and our family's hope, has become God's glorious story of His faithfulness, triumph, and victory. What the enemy intended for harm God has used to accomplish His destiny of goodness in my family's life as well as encourage those He allows us to share our story with—all for God's glory (Genesis 50:20).

As for me, twenty-six years later, I have truly found the contagiousness of my parents' faith in Jesus and God's Word. His Word is life. I continue to live daily with eyes wide open, as I seek and love Jesus first and recognize His whereabouts in life's wild adventures. My life's journey can be described in the lyrics of the song, "Graves Into Gardens" by Brandon Lake and Elevation Worship along with the joy described in the melody, "The Goodness of God" by Bethel Music. I have discovered, knowing God's presence is with me changes the way I go through anything and everything. He is my hope and goodness in every season of life.

I have since remarried a man after God's heart. Joe and I will be celebrating our fifteen-year wedding anniversary this year. We have both encountered God's miraculous transformation so profoundly in our lives. Jesus has changed everything about who we are, taking our old lives riddled with pain and addiction to a new life filled with joy, wholeness, and freedom! This life-changing transformation in our family has brought God-adventures to each season—a calling to the ministry, opportunities to share the love of Jesus in our everyday lives, and our most recent opportunity: to be Jesus School students in Orlando, Florida.

What about you? Are you ready and willing to see God's view in your *going through* with eyes wide open? I promise, it's worth it. As you conclude with the following reflection questions, I want to leave you with God's powerful and profound promise to you found in Romans 8:31–39 (MSG). As you read it, I pray your heart absorbs the truth of His love for you, that you seize this promise and make it yours as you make your request: *Lord, open my eyes so that I may see what You see.* He is faithful to provide you: eyes wide open.

So, what do you think? With God on our side like this, how can we lose? If God didn't hesitate to put everything on the line for us, embracing our condition and exposing himself to the worst by sending his own Son, is there anything else he wouldn't gladly and freely do for us? And who would dare tangle with God by messing with one of God's chosen? Who would dare even to point a finger? The One who died for us—who was raised to life for us!—is in the presence of God at this very moment sticking up for us. Do you think anyone is going to be able to drive a wedge between us and Christ's love for us? There is no way! Not trouble, not hard times, not hatred, not hunger, not homelessness, not bullying threats, not

backstabbing, not even the worst sins listed in Scripture:

> They kill us in cold blood because they hate you. We're
>
> sitting ducks; they pick us off one by one.

None of this fazes us because Jesus loves us. I'm absolutely

convinced that nothing—nothing living or dead, angelic or

demonic, today or tomorrow, high or low, thinkable or

unthinkable—absolutely *nothing* can get between us and God's

love because of the way that Jesus our Master has embraced us.

(Romans 8:31–39 MSG)

Reflection Questions:

What has been your view in your *going through*? Please feel free to be real and raw with the Lord. He's not turned off by your honesty. Write down the way you have seen the details of your *going through* season on the lines below.

____

____

____

____

____

____

____

____

____

____

____

How has it *felt* to have this perspective?

What has the *going through* confronted in you?

Are you at a place now where you are desperate to see from God's view and

encounter His presence in your *going through*? Why or why not?

____

____

____

____

____

____

____

____

____

____

____

Whether you're ready or not, I want to encourage you to read and meditate on the stories of others, the lives of people, like you and I, who have traveled along in wild seasons of *going through*. I believe as you read and meditate on God's Word, the powerful and personal presence of the Holy Spirit will do in you exactly what you desire most right now. As you read the following narratives—Exodus 33, Joshua 1–3, Daniel, 1 Samuel 17, Ruth, Nehemiah, Acts 12, and Acts 16—answer the following questions: What kind of season or situation were they *going through*? What were they facing that was challenging, difficult, and disheartening? Where was God in their *going through*? Could they see Him or from His view? How did the Lord provide them with eyes wide open? Share your findings on the lines below and write down discoveries that you are seeing in your *going through* season by reading theirs.

____

____

____

____

____

____

Are you ready to be still with Him and receive His insight? Psalm 46:10 reminds us to be still and know that He is God. As you sit with Him, allow the Holy Spirit to meet you right where you are. Take time to ponder His presence in your *going through* while you worship Him to a few melodies that will remind you of His whereabouts: "You Get the Glory" by Jonathan Traylor; "Armies" by KB; "Whom Shall I Fear (God of Angel Armies)" by Chris Tomlin; "Yes Song" by KB; "Way Maker" by Jesus Image, John Wilds, and Steffany Gretzinger; "Lost in Your Love" by Brandon Lake; and "Goodness of God" by Bethel Music. The Lord wants to pour out His love on you (Romans 5:5). He desires to bring you His view (Psalm 103:7). His perspective and presence are available to you as you sit at His feet in full surrender (Isaiah 55:6, 8–9). As you rest with Him, how is He providing you with eyes wide open?

____

____

____

____

____

____

I want to leave you with some life-giving encouragement—God's promise of eyes wide open. His whereabouts in your *going through*. His presence in your uncertainties. His perspective that you receive through His Spirit. Hold on to them tightly, with a faith-filled grip. They are His words and His promises as He reminds you of His omnipresence, His sovereignty, and His omniscient goodness in your *going through*.

- First Corinthians 2:9–12 (NLT) says, "That is what the Scriptures mean when they say, 'No eye has seen, no ear has heard, and no mind has imagined what God has prepared for those who love him.' But it was to us that God revealed these things by his Spirit. For his Spirit searches out everything and shows us God's deep secrets. No one can know a person's thoughts except that person's own spirit, and no one can know God's thoughts except God's own Spirit. And we have received God's Spirit (not the world's spirit), so we can know the wonderful things God has freely given us."

- Proverbs 2:3–6 (AMP) says, "Yes, if you cry out for insight, and lift up your voice for understanding; if you seek skillful and godly wisdom as you would silver and search for her as you would hidden treasures; then you will understand the [reverent] fear of the LORD [that is, worshiping

Him and regarding Him as truly awesome] and discover the knowledge of God. For the LORD gives [skillful and godly] wisdom; from His mouth come knowledge and understanding."

- Isaiah 43:1–3 (NLT) says, "But now, O Jacob, listen to the LORD who created you. O Israel, the one who formed you says, 'Do not be afraid, for I have ransomed you. I have called you by name; you are mine. When you go through deep waters, I will be with you. When you go through rivers of difficulty, you will not drown. When you walk through the fire of oppression, you will not be burned up; the flames will not consume you. For I am the LORD, your God, the Holy One of Israel, your Savior.'"

- First Corinthians 2:14–16 (MSG) says, "The unspiritual self, just as it is by nature, can't receive the gifts of God's Spirit. There's no capacity for them. They seem like so much silliness. Spirit can be known only by spirit—God's Spirit and our spirits in open communion. Spiritually alive, we have access to everything God's Spirit is doing, and can't be judged by unspiritual critics. Isaiah's question, 'Is there anyone around who knows God's Spirit, anyone who knows what he is doing?' has been answered: Christ knows, and we have Christ's Spirit."

CONCLUSION

As we say farewell for now, my hope is that you have discovered the One who is right here with you in your *going through*. He is the One who holds your hand through the stages of grief and dismay. He's the One who pursues your heart in the chaos of your pain. He is the One who never leaves you nor forsakes you, regardless of your pushback. He's the One who *goes through* with you, even when it feels like the world is moving on without you. This One is Jesus.

Jesus is in the fight and the flight. He is your security, even while you're searching for safekeeping. He is in the difficult and challenging moments of your waiting. He is the mender of your broken heart. He is in control, even when you've lost all control. He's the void filler of your unfulfilled chasms and despairing gaps. He is the chain breaker, the One who sets the prisoners free. He is the One who is sovereign, omniscient, and omnipresent. He gives His perspective—giving you eyes wide open—in the midst of your tough times. Embrace Him as you *go through*. He will not disappoint.

My heart's desire is that you have encountered the personal love, grace, presence, and goodness of Jesus through the pages of this devotional. I know that reflecting on the trials, digging deep, and searching your soul is difficult.

However, I truly believe, with God's divine insight, it changes everything about the *going through*. My prayer is that you know, believe, and seize every single promise in God's Word for you and that you experience all that He has for you—His salvation, His healing, His freedom, His victory, and His love—during your tough times.

If you haven't accepted Jesus as your Lord and Savior yet, or if you know deep down that you've walked away from Him and placed Him on the back burner of your life—maybe He's someone you used to know but He's become secondary to other things in your life; perhaps you've been distracted or hurt by religion, or maybe you feel as though God has let you down—whatever the situation or reason, I want you to know something: God is love (1 John 4:16). He is the real-deal, downright definition of love. And His love for you is ridiculously extraordinary. His love desires to meet you exactly where you are right at this very moment.

God knew your name before you were born, and He chose you (Jeremiah 1:5). Plus, He knows everything about you (Psalm 139) and still loves you. He is madly in love with you, and nothing can stop Him from loving you (Romans 8:38–39). He has been pursuing you every step of the way and He will not let go, no matter what (Psalm 139:7–12). In fact, He takes great delight in you, and His love and rejoicing over you speaks His destiny and identity about you (Zephaniah 3:17). God sent His only Son, Jesus, to take your place, to cover your pain, mistakes, hurts, and struggles (John 3:16), and He came to give you abundant life in Him (John 10:10); a life that goes beyond your *going through*. He's calling you to find life in Him alone (John 1:4) as His Spirit, the Holy Spirit, draws you to Him (John 15:26). Why? Because He loves you exponentially! He loved you first (1 John 4:19) and His is a love worth living for because His love unselfishly died in your place to give you a real and fulfilling life in Him (Romans 5:8)!

Recently, the Lord gave me a personal perspective of what His sacrifice at the cross looked like (John 19). I pray, as I share, it helps you to see His remarkable love for yourself, as I have seen it for myself. My vision revealed an image of Roman soldiers whipping Jesus. As the soldiers flogged Him, they shouted, "This is for Jodi!" Every blow bore *my* name. Every lash had *my* name attached to it. My name from their mouths shamed and crushed my spirit. These images connected to *my* name continued to flash before my mind's eye sharply and repeatedly: the crown of thorns crushing into His skull, the careless plucking and pulling out of His beard, the driving of iron nails into His hands and feet while He was placed on the cross; the forceful spear piercing His side. "This is for Jodi!" *My* name was stamped to His torture and thrust upon Him as a weight He did not deserve to carry. I wept and felt grieved by these personalized pictures that ran through my thoughts. *Yet* Jesus stayed silent: He would not stop the soldiers. I could see Him as the Lamb led to the slaughter without a complaint or a defense (Isaiah 53:7). He endured every part of the torture and chaos, attached to *my* name, in humility and extravagant love.

As I continued to cry with gratitude and great repentance, He began to reveal a new image to me. This updated view presented a whole, fully alive Jesus—walking out of the same grave that *my* name put Him in. While Jesus walked out, He shouted in a loud victorious cry of triumph and joyful celebration: "This is for Jodi!" It was *then* I could truly see the real reason my name was fastened to His sacrifice. Jesus, the Lamb of God, was slaughtered in silence for my sin, my pain, my sickness, and my *going through,* while Jesus, the Lion of Judah, conquered it all for me and won the complete victory over my *going through* (Revelation 5:5). This is true love, displayed for you and for me (John 15:9–13).

If your heart is hungry for Jesus, the One who loves you extravagantly and the One who's taken me through the wild ride of this crazy life, I'd love to pray with you to receive all of Him. Before we do, please take a moment to read His invitation to you in Isaiah 55. Take some time to meditate on the price His love has paid for you, as Isaiah 53 describes. Our names were attached to His death, but our names were shouted from His lips in victory as He overcame *our* sin, death, sickness, heartache, and pain. As we pray, lay it all down, surrender all of you—the good, the bad, and the ugly. Admit your desperation for Him and receive His unconditional love for you. It's as simple as a heartfelt, genuine prayer to Him.

Dear Jesus, I need You. I'm desperate for You. I'm sorry. Thank You for paying the price for my life with Your life. I believe You are the Son of God and that You removed my sins with Your blood and sacrifice. Thank You, Jesus. Please come into my heart, transform me, and make me new in You. In Jesus's name, amen.

A decision like this requires a serious celebration! In case you don't know, heaven is rejoicing because of your decision to surrender your all to Jesus (Luke 15:8–10 MSG), so why don't we join them! Take time to listen to "King of Kings" by Jesus Image and sing your heart out to Him with gratitude while praising and worshipping your *new* King! The One who paid it all for you and The One who has given you the victory!

Because you have now received Jesus as your Lord and Savior, you get everything He paid for on the cross and through His resurrection (1 Peter 1:3–7; 2

Peter 1:3–4)! You are also sealed by His Spirit, the Holy Spirit (Ephesians 1:13–14). Every promise God makes in His Word is yes and amen for you (2 Corinthians 1:20)!

As you take each day with Him, be sure to spend personal time alone with Him. Read His Word daily; thank Him, praise Him, worship Him, and enjoy His friendship and presence. His Word is your food for life, while your praise and adoration toward Him is His food (Numbers 28:2). It is vital that you live your life in His Word and in His presence: it's where your new life is found (Titus 3:5). His Spirit, the Holy Spirit is your extraordinary gift from God Himself and it's His first installment that guarantees everything God has promised you (Acts 2:38; 2 Corinthians 1:22). You must find Him daily in the secret place (Psalm 27 and Psalm 91). The secret place is your alone time with Jesus, where you love on Him and listen to Him and spend quality time in His Word and in His glorious presence. As you do this, your daily life will be full of exuberant joy by His Spirit (Nehemiah 8:10; Psalm 16:11; Luke 10:21; Acts 13:52) and supernatural peace and power (Acts 1:8; Philippians 4:6–7; Galatians 5:22-23)! Take some time to listen to "Talking to Jesus" by Elevation Worship and Maverick City Music. It will encourage your understanding of how special this secret place with Jesus really is.

Here's a few of my favorite Bible reading recommendations as you open His love letter to you—go through the Gospels: Matthew, Mark, Luke, and John. Put yourself in each scene while you follow Jesus's steps and His stops. Listen to His words while you ask the Holy Spirit to reveal His understanding to you with each and every word. Follow the first church through the book of Acts; you'll see the powerful actions of the Holy Spirit and how God's power moved in love and unity among God's people. Wherever you dive in first, whether it's Esther, Daniel, Isaiah, Genesis, Joshua, 1 Corinthians, or Revelation, you will always find Jesus, Your Savior, in every detail of every book in God's Word.

Another important step for you is to get water baptized as Jesus demonstrated and instructed us to do in Matthew 3:11, Mark 16:16, and Matthew 28:19–20. Something powerful takes place in you and through you, in that water, as you fully surrender, submit, and obey Jesus's instructions. A freedom takes place that breaks every chain. Also, find a church home that teaches the Word of God, from the beginning to the end and everything in between. This should be a place that encourages you to run after Jesus, to hunger and thirst for more of Him, and to surround yourself with people who will sharpen your faith to new levels (Hebrews 10:25)!

Next, ask Jesus to fill you up with His supernatural power. This power will empower and equip you to do life with Jesus (Galatians 5; Hebrews 13:21; John 7:38–39). The Holy Spirit's fiery authority in you will strengthen, authorize, and train you to do life lavishly in love with Jesus and to share His love with others (Acts 10:38). Which leads me to the next and final step for you to take— share with others what Jesus has done and is doing in you (Acts 4:8). His blood was shed for your new life in Him! Hebrews 9:14 (ERV) says, "So surely the blood sacrifice of Christ can do much more. Christ offered himself through the eternal Spirit as a perfect sacrifice to God. His blood will make us completely clean from the evil we have done. It will give us clear consciences so that we can worship the living God." As you share with others what Jesus has paid for with His blood, it has deep impact that will blow your mind and others! Revelation 12:11 (GW) says, "They won the victory over him because of the blood of the lamb and the word of their testimony. They didn't love their life so much that they refused to give it up." There is power and victory in the blood of Jesus that was shed for your life, and that same power and victory from the blood of Jesus operates like a ferocious, full-blown locomotive with great intention and supernatural force through the word of *your* testimony about Jesus! So, don't hold back! Share His life, death, and resurrection with others every chance you get.

Aside from your daily Bible reading, I'd also love to recommend a few books by authors who will encourage you as you run after Jesus. *The Jesus Book: Fall Recklessly in Love with Jesus* as well as *Holy Spirit: The One Who Makes Jesus Real*, both by Michael Koulianos, will reveal with spectacular insight who Jesus is and the One who makes Jesus real. *Crazy Love: Overwhelmed by a Relentless God* by Francis Chan, *Good Morning, Holy Spirit* by Benny Hinn, *The Pursuit of God: The Human Thirst for The Divine* by A. W. Tozer, *My All for Him: Fall in love with Jesus all over again* by Basilea Schlink and *A Tale of Three Kings: A Study in Brokenness* by Gene Edwards will also rev up your faith and stir your heart with hunger for more of Jesus while receiving insight on the love of God, encouraging you to live out your faith with great joy, boldness, and enthusiasm.

I truly hope my journey has helped and encouraged you in yours and perhaps at times made you smile or maybe even laugh, but most importantly, I hope it's allowed you to see that you are not alone in your *going through*. Jesus is with you. Anytime you find yourself *going through* another tough time, or if you know of a friend or even a stranger who is facing the pains of a difficult season, please meet me back here and share this devotional with them. We will all *go through*—together—with Jesus holding our hand.

As we close, I want to encourage you with two more songs: "You're Gonna Be Okay" by Brian and Jenn Johnson and "You Make Me Brave" by Amanda Cook and Bethel Music. As you listen and absorb every word, I pray your soul grasps the truth of each and every lyric; they are foundational statements found in God's Word, and they are for *you*. Also, if this devotional has encouraged you through your journey, leaving an Amazon review substantially helps to share this book with others who are also *going through*. Because I self-publish, I don't have a company sharing my story with others; instead, it's all word of mouth, so a review from you speaks powerfully to other readers in search of the hope that only Jesus Christ can bring. Your thoughts on this devotional may highlight your positive experience and draw people to Jesus who need hope in their difficult season.

Lastly, I want to leave you with these beautiful, powerful, and stick-to-the rib expressions from Jesus found in John 16:33. May they encourage you as you meditate on their truth, rest in their power, and surrender to their provision. And may you fully discover and understand: Hope has a name; His name is Jesus. I pray you find the presence of Hope in the tough times of your *going through* and that His victory will be proclaimed over your tragedy.

I have told you these things, so that in Me you may have [perfect]

peace. In the world you have tribulation and distress and suffering,

but be courageous [be confident, be undaunted, be filled with joy];

I have overcome the world. [My conquest is accomplished, My

victory abiding.]

(John 16:33 AMP)

ACKNOWLEDGMENTS

I can't tell you how many times over the last fifteen years I've tried writing my *going through* story. It seemed like every time I sat down to type the details on my computer, in the quietness of my comforting home, the words were just that—words. I knew without the Holy Spirit's presence, power, anointing, and leading with my words, this story would be . . . just words. And that's something I'm not interested in. I don't care about my words; I care about *His* words. So, over the last fifteen years, I have found myself setting this manuscript aside, surrendering it to the Lord, time and time again.

It wasn't until this season, twenty-six years after the shooting, I felt the Holy Spirit's gentle whisper to my heart say, *It's time*. As I began to write, His presence, His anointing, His power, and His leading began to spill out from every single word I typed. Every page and every chapter flowed from my personal and precious time with Him. So, as I close, please know, these words are not just my words but *His* words of encouragement and love to you.

I want to shout a great thank-you with sincere gratitude to the Holy Spirit for leading me through this special time of writing with Him. I have never understood why I love to write so much, especially since I have never thought of myself as gifted with any special talent. However, I've discovered through this process the real reason why I love to write. It is a wonderful privilege and an incredible joy to partner with You, Holy Spirit, as You graciously give me opportunities to do so. Writing with You brings life and sustenance to every word, taking this writing thing to a whole new level of exhilaration with purpose. Thank You. Oh, what a joy it has been! As You have led me through the writing process of my *going through* journey, it has been such an exquisite time together. Your presence, Your touch, Your insight—it changes everything!

Thank You, Jesus, for being my constant. Thank You for paying the price on the cross so that I can receive all that You died to give me. Every promise You made You are faithful to fulfill. You have poured out every precise word of this devotional into the depths of my heart for such a time as this. Thank You for being with me every step of the way, holding my hand, through the wild seasons of life, including the *going through*. As I share with others my personal journey with You in every single detail, I want to thank You for encouraging and helping others in theirs. You held my hand patiently and lovingly with each step of my *going through*. You walked with me *through* the pain and the healing—never, ever once leaving my side. Thank You for being true to Your Word and true to Your character; You are truly the meaning of grace, love, and hope. Thank You for loving me lavishly while *going through* with me. Jesus, You are my "One thing" (as Mary of Bethany found You when she sat at Your feet), and I love You unreservedly. Your persistent and tenacious love changes everything about the *going through*. May each reader who reads this book find You, the One they truly desire and desperately need.

Joe and Sofia, thank you for being my tribe. I'm so grateful to call you my husband, Joe. I'm so thankful to call you my daughter, Sof. Your consistent love and encouragement sharpen me every single day. Thank you for being my cheering section in life. Thank you for believing in God's destiny over my life. Thank you for making me laugh always, for adventuring through life with me, and for being my tribe through it all. I love you two with all my heart, more than words could ever express. *See you tomorrow!*

Thank you, Joe, for always running, full speed ahead, toward Jesus. You never waver or wander away. You are focused and fixed on the King of Kings. You have a heart after Jesus. You have a hunger and a thirst for more and more of Him; it is contagious to Sof and me. Thank you for leading us directly to Him. Thank you for loving me unconditionally. Thank you for being my best friend, my encourager, my building-up helper, my sharpening iron, and my joyful, hilarious adventure partner. Every season with you since 2004 has been beautiful and extraordinary; however, this season has been extra special as we have diligently sought Jesus first with greater faith, together, in ways we've only dreamed of. The Lord whispered to your heart in the fall of 2020, *It's just the beginning,* and since then our hearts have been expectant and excited as we've seen firsthand the fulfillment of His promises. Thank you for living out the meaning of Matthew 6:33 (ERV), "What you should want most is God's kingdom and doing what he wants you to do. Then he will give you all these other things you need." I love you, Joemama, always and forever. Thank you for loving me with honor, authenticity, and extravagance. I'm incredibly blessed to be your wife.

Sweet Sof, thank you. Your life brought me back to Jesus, and I will forever be grateful for God's gift of salvation and love I discovered from you. Your kind, gentle, and compassionate spirit speaks God's heart profoundly. His joy in you flows to every person around you. The Lord's hand has been on your life since day one. I can see Him moving in your life and through every detail. As you *go through* this life, His Word will direct your every step and every path, and His Spirit will be with you, on you, and all around you. And His love will intently pursue you every step of the way. Embrace every moment with Jesus. Surrender and yield to His leading. Run after Him. He will not disappoint or leave you.

Remember Proverbs 3:5–6 (AMP), "Trust in and rely confidently on the LORD with all your heart and do not rely on your own insight or understanding. In all your ways know and acknowledge and recognize Him, and He will make your paths straight and smooth [removing obstacles that block your way]." I love you, Boo, forever and always. You are a precious treasure to me from the Lord. I value and cherish you with my life.

Mom and Dad, I am beyond blessed to be your kid. I know I gave you both a run for your money, so to speak, but you loved me through it all. Thank you for your contagious faith amid my wavering. Thank you for your prayers and for reflecting the heart of God toward me always. I believe those two intentional actions of yours have influenced why I am a fully surrendered follower of Jesus today—enamored by His love and enthralled with His Word. Thank you for being the most beautiful example of Jesus to me. Thank you for living out your faith with action. It has been foundational in me and our entire family. You have lived with a hungry heart after God's heart my entire life. You have faced more *going through* seasons than anyone I have ever known, yet your lives sing of the goodness of God. Thank you for every prayer spoken over me, especially during my dark times. Thank you for standing in the gap of my pain and speaking God's destiny over me. Thank you for doing life with me and pointing me directly to the

One I have always desperately needed—Jesus! Your love, kindness, generosity, mercy, and compassion reflect the very heart of God. In a world full of pointing fingers and getting tossed aside, you continually held me up in prayer with words of love, sharing the gold God saw in me, and speaking God's purpose over me. You refused to give up on me, and for that I am eternally grateful. You revealed the love of the Father toward me (1 Corinthians 13:4–8) and the persistence and patience of His heart for me (2 Peter 3:9). I'm so thankful for your mentorship, discipleship, and investment in my life. Your lives have reflected the promise and truth of Daniel 12:3 (GW): "Those who are wise will shine like the brightness on the horizon. Those who lead many people to righteousness will shine like the stars forever and ever." Thank you for leading me, and so many, to righteousness. Thank you for helping me to tell this story—*God's* story in *our* story—may it overflow with Jesus, our hope in the tough times. I love you both so very, very, very much. Thank you for loving me.

My siblings, I love you guys! Thank you for *going through* with me. I know that each of us, though together, has faced this challenge in our own unique way. Each of us has our own *going through* story that speaks of God's faithfulness abounding even in the darkest moments. Your stories have strengthened me and inspired me to write mine. Thank you. Your friendship and hearts after Jesus have sharpened me in ways that I cannot fully articulate. I have

seen God's presence and power in each one of you. I have seen God's qualities

abound in and through you and your families. It's been an absolute joy watching

His personality shine through you as we have grown. Greg, the joy of the Lord is

your strength (Nehemiah 8:10). Jen, the peace of God exceeds your understanding

(Philippians 4:6–7). Leah, God provides everything you need (Philippians 4:19).

Thank you for being you, individual and wonderful you. I love you guys dearly.

Pastor Michael and Jess Koulianos, thank you for being our pastors and

our shepherds. It's difficult to fully describe my gratitude in words, but I'll try.

Your sacrifice has been quite costly for you and your family; however, there is a

resounding shaking in heaven as it rejoices while hell mourns because of your

exceptional sacrifice. I am just one individual among many (too numerous to

count) whom you've sharpened, encouraged, rallied, and cheered on to run after

Jesus at full speed. Thank you. Thank you. Thank you. Thank you for leading us

straight to Jesus. Thank you for staying foundational to the Word of God. Thank

you for honoring and treasuring our precious time together as a church family in

holy communion and life-giving baptism. Thank you for being real, authentic,

funny, sincere, confrontational in love, and joyful in Jesus. Thank you for

reflecting His heart in word and deed to Joe and me, as well as our entire church family worldwide. Thank you for being Spirit-led always. His presence is unlike anything else. It has changed me profoundly over these last two years. Thank you. Our time of worship together as His bride stirs me to fall more in love with Jesus. Thank you for this. Thank you for stewarding His presence and for welcoming Him to wreck each one of us, without the restraint of a clock. Thank you for loving us enough to tell us the truth. Thank you for sharing God's heart with us and allowing your mentors and friends to share their heart after the Lord with all of us—John Wilds, Pastor Benny Hinn, Ben Fitzgerald, Pastor Bill Johnson, Heidi Baker, Brother Yun, Pastor Tommy Reid, Randy Clark, Jeremy Riddle, Steffany Gretzinger, Pastor Randy Needham, Francis Chan, John Bevere, Pastors Michael and Lorisa Miller, Chase and Lindy Cofer, Brian Guerin, Pastor Paul Teske, Mike Bickle, and many more. Thank you for honoring God and honoring others. Thank you for your books, *The Jesus Book: Fall Recklessly in Love with Jesus* and *Holy Spirit: The One Who Makes Jesus Real*. They have reinforced God's Word in my heart profoundly. Thank you for teaching me how to live out Luke 10:42 (ERV) daily, in word and deed: "Only one thing is important. Mary has made the right choice, and it will never be taken away from her." Thank you. Thank you. Thank you. Joe and I are incredibly blessed and thankful to be students at Jesus School. We're excited, full of childlike faith, running after the

One who is worthy of it all! Thank you, PMK and Jess, for everything. We love you, we cherish you, and we honor you. You are priceless and precious to the kingdom of heaven.

My Jesus Image Church family, thank you! Joe and I moved across the country two years ago, from Michigan to Florida. We left quite a bit behind, including our "dream" jobs, our comfortable home and lives, family, friends, and the church where we began pursuing the Lord together. It was the place Joe and I were most comfortable; we had the wonderful privilege of doing life with many familiar people whom we loved dearly. As the Lord called us to a new chapter, we said our good-byes to the familiar and the comfortable, and we knew this letting go was just the beginning, but the Lord was directing our every step. We had no clue, no agenda, and no clear direction for what the Lord was up to. We only knew one thing, and we recognized it our first month as residents of Florida. We visited Jesus Image in September 2020. It was then that we knew that we knew that we knew: Jesus Image was our new church home. Although we were living three hours away at the time, it was worth every trip. To be in the house of the Lord with hungry, thirsty people who wanted more of Jesus was where we knew we wanted to be. Thank you for welcoming us. Thank you for beautifully revealing the bride of Christ, His church. Thank you for stewarding God's presence authentically and sincerely. Thank you for making everything about Jesus. Thank you for shining the love of Jesus profoundly not only to Joe and me but to the entire world. Jesus Image Church, you exemplify Matthew 5:14–16 (MSG), "Here's another way to put it: You're here to be light, bringing out the God-colors in the world. God is not a secret to be kept. We're going public with this, as public as a city on a hill. If I make you light-bearers, you don't think I'm going to hide you under a bucket, do you? I'm putting you on a light stand. Now that I've put you there on a hilltop, on a light stand—shine! Keep open house; be generous with your lives. By opening up to others, you'll prompt people to open up with God, this generous Father in heaven." Thank you to each one of you. We love you. Thank you for loving us so well.

Shawn Bolz, thank you for your timely ministry. I've had the beautiful privilege to see from a whole new lens through your teachings and books over the last few years. I'll never forget reading your book *Translating God: Hearing God's Voice for Yourself and the World Around You* and the Lord highlighting 1 Corinthians 14:1 (NLT) to me from the pages for the first time: "Let love be your highest goal! But you should also desire the special abilities the Spirit gives— especially the ability to prophesy." This verse sent me on a distinct expedition of understanding God's love for me through His Word while learning to share His love creatively with others as the Holy Spirit leads me. It's helped me to see and understand my true calling in life, as reflected in Matthew 22:37–39 (NLT): "Jesus replied, '"You must love the LORD your God with all your heart, all your soul, and all your mind." This is the first and greatest commandment. A second is equally important: "Love your neighbor as yourself."'" This reveals why I receive such tremendous joy as I love Him first and then share His love with others. Thank you. Thank you for providing opportunities for me to learn from your Jesus-friends—Steve and Ginny Maddox as well as Bob and Lauren Hasson. They, too, have encouraged me immensely in my journey as I have begun to understand God's supernatural ways of communicating and leading. I wake up excited every day to run after Jesus and see Him in my everyday details, in the marketplace, and beyond. I'm blown away by His willingness to partner with little ole me. Thank you, Shawn, for your ministry and words of life and for cheering me on through this season!

Aston Gardens friends, thank you for your friendship. Thank you for being my family. What a privilege and honor it was to do life with you. You welcomed me into Florida with refreshing kindness, consideration, and thoughtfulness. Each and every day you brought laughter, humor, hilarity, and joy! I have learned so much in our special season from each of you. There are too many of you to name here, but you know who you are. Thank you for allowing me to be a part of your everyday lives. Thank you for the daily encouragement, hugs, and smiles. Thank you for the wisdom shared and for the opportunities to serve you. Thank you for the heartfelt talks and times we've shed tears together, even over a good-bye. Thank you for allowing me to sing to you down the hallways and for putting up with my silly dance moves in the lobby. Thank you for the giggles we've shared over Pictionary, Brain Games, and Jeopardy. Thank you for impacting my life in ways that I can't fully put into words. My Bible study friends, thank you for learning with me as we studied God's Word together. It has been an honor and a great blessing to teach and to study God's Word with you, to encourage one another in our faith and to do life with one another. I'm thankful that the Lord opened up this time for us to grow together. Our times together each week were providential and sweet, full of joy and full of fun and uplifting truths. Thank you for being my precious family and my Jesus-loving friends. Keep digging in and running full speed ahead after Jesus (Matthew 6:33). My Bingo friends, thank you for allowing me to make Bingo a circus act (ha-ha!). Every pattern became something fun! I have loved watching the joy you receive in playing. Thank you for letting me join the fun. Also, thank you for the wonderful privilege to edit *The Gazette* for our AG community. Thank you for loving me and accepting me as me. I love each one of you, and I'm so grateful that God provided me the special privilege to know you and do life with you.

Deb Hall, my editor, thank you for your wisdom and expertise. You bring so much joy to the entire writing and editing process. You are always willing to answer a question, share sensible counsel, and encourage me in every step. Thank you. I'm very grateful to have you be a part of my manuscripts. What a blessing and a godsend you are. You use God's gift in you so beautifully, just as 1 Peter 4:10–11 (GW) speaks of: "Each of you as a good manager must use the gift that God has given you to serve others. Whoever speaks must speak God's words. Whoever serves must serve with the strength God supplies so that in every way God receives glory through Jesus Christ. Glory and power belong to Jesus Christ forever and ever! Amen." Thank you, Deb. I appreciate you.

Last but not least, to those who were a part of my *going through* season—thank you. Looking back, I can see how much I learned from each one of you. You walked through this crisis with our family. It was messy, painful, scary, and dark, but that didn't stop you. You generously loved, supported, encouraged, and helped our family without hesitation. You responded just as Jesus would. Thank you for being the hands and feet of Jesus so exquisitely. There are too many of you to name, but you know who you are. Thank you to our Milford Assembly of

God church family, along with the Michigan District of the Assemblies of God, plus our Milford community of friends and essential service workers. Thank you to the first responders who played a pivotal and essential role in assisting our family—the police and task force along with Huron Valley Hospital's medical staff. Thank you. Thank you to all of you for reflecting God's heart to me and my family in a time of turmoil, confusion, and pain. Jesus in you impacted who I am today. Thank you for living out Galatians 6:2 (AMP) to the tee: "Carry one another's burdens and in this way you will fulfill the requirements of the law of Christ [that is, the law of Christian love]." Thank you for *going through* with me.